Urban Economic Anatomy
Upheaval & Change in Detroit

by
John F. Sase, Ph.D.

Urban Economic Anatomy
Upheaval & Change in Detroit

© ® 2009, John F. Sase

Urban Economic Anatomy
Upheaval & Change in Detroit

A Project of Kavish Media Group Economic Series
SASE Associates

by
John F. Sase, Ph.D.

with
Gerard J. Senick, contributing editor

and
Patrick T. Halley (dec.), researcher/journalist

ISBN is 1449510116
EAN-13 is 9781449510114

Address inquiries to
drjohn@saseassociates.com
SASE Associates
27350 Southfield Rd. PMB 170
Lathrup Village, MI 48076

Dedication

This and subsequent volumes are dedicated to the memory of Patrick T. Halley, a member of our editorial team who passed away suddenly and tragically in 2007. A writer, playwright, director, and actor who formerly was the Cultural Editor of the *Fifth Estate* newspaper in Detroit, Pat was a gifted journalist who combined hard facts and wicked humor in a particularly insightful and entertaining manner. His awareness of politics and culture and perceptive analysis of them, affection for Detroit and its citizens, and clever jibes and use of wordplay will be sorely missed.

This volume is the first in a planned series. The work represents the outcome of my monthly column in the Detroit/Oakland County Legal News. In my eleven years working on that series, I muse and reflect on the great English economist John Stuart Mill who published some of his most influential and socially important pieces in *Fraser's Magazine for Town and Country*, London, England, during the mid-nineteenth century (see the Afterglow for Economists at the end of this volume).

In this first volume, we have focused on a number of major current issues in the field of Urban Economics. Specifically, we have addressed the economic upheaval and change facing Detroit, Michigan during the decline of its industrial age and, most immediately, the demise of the automotive industry—at least as we have known it. Like a red phoenix regenerating itself the city may once again rise from its ashes and enter its next phase of development.

--Dr. John Sase

Prelude

To Rebuild a City: Economic Anatomy 101

"If You Seek a Pleasant Peninsula, Look about You."[1]

Most of us agree that Detroit needs fixing. Numerous and vast tracts of land in the city must be cleaned up and redeveloped. In order to better serve the Tri-County Area, public utilities, including transportation, water, and sewerage, require reorganization.

When talking about such a massive redevelopment project, one may think in terms of a blank slate. However, such a canvas does not exist, nor has it ever existed. Going to an analogy of the other extreme, sifting through a mass of what may appear to be haphazard growth over the past century leaves us with confusion--not seeing the forest for the trees.

When we allow ourselves the power to see beyond clutter and popular myths, we gain the ability to view the site through the portal of our history, thus finding the underlying order beneath. Finding this order within the chaos derives from the practice of Economic Anatomy.

In this volume, we will look at the anatomy of Detroit—not only its geography, but its early growth and development from antiquity to the present. By doing this, we hope to refute common myths, show the evolution of our city, and suggest a way to prepare for rebuilding it. Only by understanding our past can we move effectively into our future.

Loup-Garou Sez, "If You Seek a Pleasant Swamp…"

How deep should we dig and how fundamentally should we look to understand the "what and why" of our development? No matter how shallow or deep we choose to go, our first task is to erase the artificial separations of counties and municipalities from our minds in order to view the territory as a whole. What we find in the Tri-County Area is a large lake plain bordered on the northwest by the hilly edge of a glacial moraine left after the last Ice Age. The ice sheets receded from the region on a peninsula (the Mitten), leaving many lakes and numerous major river systems.

Okay, we know what the lay of the land looks like. However, how have we developed it? To understand fully the complex layers of this matter, we must search the Pre-Columbian roots of Detroit. Over the past century and a half, researchers such as archaeologists W. K. Moorehead and W. B. Hinsdale, building upon the earlier work of surveyor/geologists Bela Hubbard and Douglas Houghton, pieced together a significant amount of our ancient history.

First of all, let us rid ourselves of the baloney that the radial pattern of our major thoroughfares, including Michigan, Grand River, and Woodward Avenues as well as Mound Road and Gratiot, was modeled after the hub-and-spoke plans of Paris, France and Washington, D.C. Though this myth has been promulgated by urban scientists and planners in otherwise commendable books and journal articles, it is nothing but a load of balderdash. Remember the scene in the film *Back to the Future²* when Biff's car slammed into the back of the manure truck? That's close. What we know of our Pre-Columbian or, at the very least, our pre-French history indicates that these routes existed as the "old beaten paths" for one or two millenniums before European migration to the area in the seventeenth century.

Major tribes in these earlier ages encamped along or at the ends of the routes listed above. The Sauk tribe settled at the end of the trail that led to the base of Lake Michigan (Michigan Avenue aka the Old Chicago Road). Others encamped in the fertile valley in the middle of the peninsula north of Lansing near the trail that led to the middle shore of Lake Michigan. The path to which Judge Augustus Woodward lent his name because, as he said, "It went toward the woods," led to the encampment of Chief Pontiac and his predecessors. The road known as Gratiot headed northeast past the swamp of the Loup-Garou to the marshlands along the narrow straits that connect Lake Huron and Lake St. Clair. Finally, a road was named Mound because it led to the large concentration of ceremonial/burial mounds that existed in Macomb County— but more about that in a moment. The point of this discussion is that the basic underlying transportation infrastructure exists as a hub-and-spoke not because of a fanciful imitation of older cities but because the paths represent the inherent direct routes that hail our history back to an earlier civilization that we are only beginning to discover.

In Old Detroit
Most of us are young enough to remember the City of Detroit as one entity, an entity with the apparent anomalies of the cities of Highland Park and Hamtramck lodged in the middle, cities that survived separately because of a clause in the City Charter of Detroit. However, a century ago, Detroit ended at East/West Grand Boulevard. What lay beyond that perimeter--the area now incorporated into Detroit--not only was open farmland, woods, and marshes, it

was a system of twenty-six small towns, villages, and hamlets. These small settlements were engulfed during the rapid expansion that accompanied the boom of the automotive industry during the second and third decades of the last century.

However, let us pause for a moment and get our bearings before tackling this puzzle. Long before our current civilization developed on this land, other intellectually evolved beings left their marks and influenced the development of what has come after. The major earlier civilization is often referred to as the Hopewell Culture, named after Captain M. C. Hopewell. Throughout the 1890s, W. K. Moorehead excavated a site on Hopewell's farm near Chillicothe, Ohio and found a rectangular enclosure containing thirty-eight mounds attributed to the tribes of the middle Woodland Stage. More commonly, this group of early habitants is known as the Mound-Builders. They developed a vast network of ceremonial and burial mounds in the American Midwest from approximately 500 BCE onward, reaching their apex around 800 CE. This apex marked the high point of the previous warming cycle. After that time, the population of Michigan thinned as the cooling cycle commenced. Our present warming cycle began around 1800 CE.

Who were our early Michiganders? Though their origins are uncertain, Henriette Mertz, J.D., speculated that they were ancient Phoenician mariners who traveled here to mine the extremely pure and abundant copper lodes to satisfy the demands of the ancient Egyptians and Greeks.[3] Whoever they were, the Ottowa tribe called them Yam-Ko-Desh (translated as "the prairie people"). Some archeologists believe that they came to the region to mine copper, which they traded with the Mayan and Aztec cultures of Central America. Before their large population was defeated by the united forces of the Ottawas, Ojibwas, and Potawatamis, who considered the Yam-Ko-Desh as an "axis of evil," they succeeded in constructing a large number of their mounds throughout Michigan and the rest of the Midwest. Eighty-three years ago, Dr. Hinsdale wrote that, of the approximately 1100 mounds that had once existed in Michigan, only 600 remained, with the greatest concentration of fifty-seven to be found in Clinton County north of Lansing. Specifically, in the Tri-County Area of Detroit, Dr. Hinsdale asserted that the Yam-Ko-Desh built a network of forty-two mounds—twenty-five in Macomb County, twelve in Wayne County, and two in Oakland County.[4]

The existence of only two mounds in Oakland, the county that has a greater number of significant, naturally occurring elevations, may be indicative of the placement and purpose of Yam-Ko-Desh's network of mounds, one that may have risen beyond the practical to reflect ancient scientific and spiritual beliefs. We have evidence that, in various locations on our planet, cultures of that age practiced the art/science of geometric alignment to reflect the cosmologies of their culture. For example, French philologist Xavier Guichard detailed a system of twenty-four regularly spaced alignments that emanated from Alaise, an ancient meeting place northwest of Lake Geneva, Switzerland.[5] More recently, Henry Lincoln has charted the elaborate system of alignments in the Cathar region surrounding Rennes-le-Chateau in the Languedoc region of France.[6]

Unfortunately, most of the mounds in the Detroit area were destroyed in the mid-nineteenth century by local settlers who did not recognize their importance and needed to clear their farmland. Additional mounds were destroyed in the early twentieth century to make way for urban expansion. For example, the Great Mound of Delray was razed for industrial development. This mound at the junction of the Rouge and Detroit Rivers (adjacent to Ford Motor Company's Zug Island facility) stood forty feet high, 200 feet wide, and 400 feet long. It was substantially larger than a football field and twice the height of a two-story house. *Detroit News* columnist Vivian M. Baulch stated that the mound "was so packed with bones that they were easily exposed by wandering cattle."[7] In *Primitive Man in Michigan,* Hinsdale wrote that the mounds "have proven to be burial sites" and speculated that they arose from an ancient custom of having the tribes meet to honor the bones of their dead every ten to fifteen years.

Fortunately, a few mounds, such as the one beneath the governor's house on the grounds of historic Fort Wayne, remains as reminders of our ancient past. In the days when Belle Isle was still known as Hog Island, references and notations on the survey maps drawn by Bela Hubbard, Douglas Houghton, and Sylvester W. Higgins in the 1840s indicate approximate locations of some of the destroyed mounds. More curiously, many of the sites identified by Hubbard as Indian burial grounds in Detroit now have modern places of religious worship erected upon them, thus preserving some respect for their sacred heritage.

How You Gonna Keep 'Em Down on the Farm after They've Seen the Farm?

Let us return to the development of the towns, villages, and hamlets that became the City of Detroit. The remains of these sites generally are visible when they survive in the form of neighborhood retail and service areas. The suburban town centers have survived as independent communities bearing names such as Ferndale, Birmingham, Farmington, and Melvindale. However, to ferret out the vestiges of former settlements, one must search more closely in Detroit itself.

Here are a few examples of former settlements. The community of Springwells remains visible along West Vernor Highway near Springwells Avenue in southwest Detroit. Many of us remember eating treats at the Paradise ice cream and candy parlor only a few decades ago. The remains of Greenfield are visible at the corner of Greenfield and Grand River Avenues (does anyone remember Montgomery Wards, Federals, and the Norwest Theatre?) while that of Oakman can be seen in the shopping district of open and shuttered retail stores at the intersection of Oakman Boulevard and Grand River. Though few readers may recognize the names of DeBoisville or Sand Hill, many Detroiters still visit the development now called Old Redford when they come to view the classic film series at the Redford Theatre on Lahser north of West McNichols Road. Along Gratiot Avenue, the remains of Leesville and Trombley have all but disappeared, giving way to the development of Gethsemane Cemetery south of Detroit City Airport. However, further out Gratiot, the vestiges of the village of Greiner and the Connor Creek P.O. remain in the retail area from East McNichols to beyond Seven Mile Road.

In addition, many smaller settlements developed along the railway system that was built in the late nineteenth century. These clusters of a few homes, a general store with a post office, and possibly a railroad junction yard gave rise to places with names such as Oak and Yew, westward along the West Chicago and Plymouth Roads; Whitewood at Woodward and Puritan Avenues; and Norris along the rail lines near Seven Mile and Van Dyke. During the rapid expansion of the City of Detroit, these places served as hubs of development and focal points of activities as the mosaic of small family farms gave way to the early sprawl of residential subdivisions.

"I've Been Working on the Railroad"
The development of the rail lines that partitioned Wayne County in the late nineteenth century provided a major L-shaped corridor proceeding northward, parallel to Mound Road, and westward, parallel to Plymouth Road. In addition, another line running parallel to Woodward Avenue, a main trunk line running downriver, and a number of spurs leading to industrial sites along the Detroit River further partitioned the nascent cityscape into a number of large and small parcels that would host the emergence of their separate, unique cultures. In the decades preceding the construction of high-speed, limited-access freeways, ninety percent of "walk-to-work" Detroit's industry established itself along these rail lines. These industrial parks created a no-man's land that further limited access between the to-be-developed residential areas.

Down in the Hood
Decades later, during the 1950s through the 1970s, the construction of our current freeway system resulted in even smaller residential pockets being carved out of mature neighborhoods. Desirable or undesirable, the City of Detroit and the larger metropolitan area have developed as they have. The Metro area has become what it is. The isolation has hurt some neighborhoods while it seems to have helped others. From the study of neighborhoods such as Delray, we find that this isolation has led to a rapid degeneration of the area. However, in other cases, the isolation has created an incubator for new cultures to develop and thrive. For example, the West Vernor Highway area that is bounded by the Fisher Freeway on the south, the Ambassador Bridge approach on the east, and the Norfolk Southern and CN North America rail lines on the north and west houses the Holy Redeemer and Clark Park neighborhoods and has created a

5

base for the development of a thriving Latino business and residential community. To cite another example, the primary residential and business area of Hamtramck, centered at Joseph Campau Street, rests in an area contained by the CN North America line and industrial complexes on the south and east, the Chrysler Freeway to the west, and the Detroit Terminal rail line to the north. Apart from this municipality's financial woes, the City of Hamtramck continues to thrive as a Polish community as well as one that includes Eastern European, African American, and Arabic residents, among others.

As we have traced the history of Detroit, a place that has been affectionately referred to as "America's largest small town," from its ancient roots through the present, we find the emergence of a culturally rich community that is home to 125 different language groups. In addition, we find both diversity and strong cultural commonalities that reflect our distant past. The common experience has been impacted in both positive and negative ways by the lay of the land, the cooling and warming cycles, the natural routes of travel, the impact of the overlays of multiple systems of survey geometry, the development of major transportation technologies and their infrastructures, and a residential-building industry that has snowballed twice in the past century, with each episode lasting for a couple of decades. Naturally, it is enough to make anyone of us feel incredibly overwhelmed.

"We Talked with Tribal Elders on a Silver Winter's Morn"[8]
According to the real estate men and women who were active half a century ago, this development of Detroit and its environs was not haphazard. Though not formal historians, they had picked up on many of the legends described above. Having grown up in a real estate family, I listened as my father related much of the lore of the local "real estate tribe" at the dinner table throughout my childhood. He explained that some neighborhoods were planned on preferential land and that housing was designed and constructed to last four hundred years or more. On the other hand, much of the housing was erected on marginal land with design and construction intended to make these homes last through the heyday of the automotive industry—a total of sixty to eighty years. In other words, there existed a cohesive plan and long-term vision for the investment in and development of the Detroit economy that was thoroughly understood a century ago. What transpires today would be of no surprise to those on the inside track during the 1920s. In fact, the entire economic scenario has been playing out just as they had expected and related to some of us.

By retracing the paths of the Yam-Ko-Desh and the Loup-Garou, we embrace our rich cultural heritage while learning about the realities of our present living situation. Based on our Economic Anatomy lesson, we can identify the loci of redevelopment and growth. Because of the mosaic of our history, we have learned that there are many different places to invest our money, time, and energy. This knowledge will facilitate the rebuilding of our city. It helps us to understand what works (and what does not) and where best to direct investment capital. In addition, it allows us to maintain a realistic view of the structure and dynamics of the Metro area. By focusing on the microeconomic level, we can identify the best places for investment. Our Economic Anatomy lesson allows us to prioritize, organize, direct efforts, and to make sound business decisions. We can identify each area and study its context to the very heart of it. For attorneys, the rebuilding of our city may involve land use issues, deeds, titles, sales and acquisition of property, the legal rights of many different stakeholders, and personal investment. So follow the ancient path; it will lead you to the future.

Chapter 1

The New Urbanism:
Anti-Geography and the Architecture of Misery

"What ignominy! What a vile perversion of fate! That I of almost infinite capacity and uncanny grace, should perforce live unfamous and harlot-like, blundering for almost ever in these vile sewers; a sodden wreck, prey to the lascivious insect and bilious gas-clouds of persons who have never heard even one note... not even one... of the infinite music of the spheres, such a one is I, and may the rest of the world be damned for eternity!" -- The Phantom of the Opera

In the 19th Century, newspaperman Horace Greeley coined the term "Manifest Destiny" to describe the inevitability of the U. S. to expand all the way to the Pacific Ocean. Little would he suspect that in courthouses and playgrounds, and at water fountains and sewers a century later, this drama would still play itself out.

If further proof was needed that Mad Cow Disease has indeed breached our borders, one need look no further than the recent U. S. Supreme Court ruling-- and the editorial apologies for it in the Detroit *News* and the *Wall Street Journal*-- that upholds the "takings" rule as applied to wetlands protection. In this ruling, economic value is deemed to be "taken" from a property owner if government rules limit future development.

In the decision which involved a Rhode Island coastal marsh and the local efforts to protect it from development, the court said: "Future generations, too, have a right to challenge unreasonable limitations on the use and value of land."

As the Detroit *Free Press* said, incredulously: "This court ruling allows owners to make a "takings" claim no matter how much time has passed or how many other owners there have been since wetlands rules were enacted." In effect, the ruling legitimizes the recent tactic of some developers to buy up swamp land with no real intention of developing it. These developers then use a form of environmental extortion to force a township, state, or lakefront association to

9

buy the land from them for some ephemeral "market value," that is, the money that they think they deserve if they really would have developed it.

It's High Noon, and Here Come da Judge

Locally, one person who may never sleep is Lee Schwartz, the spokesman for the politically powerful Michigan Association of Home Builders. On 8 July, Schwartz went on record in the Detroit *News* as attacking a rather tepid bill that was sponsored by State Rep. Patricia Birkholtz, a Republican from Saugatuck. Called the Coordinating Planning Act bill, this bill would put gums, if not teeth, in an effort to (finally) promote some community planning in Michigan.

Birkholz's bill intends for the state to provide grant money, on a preferential basis, to townships or cities to buy up vacant land, provided such entities develop some comprehensive land-use plan.

In a response that one would expect George Armstrong Custer to give to the Sioux and Cheyenne regarding land encroachment, Schwartz, whose organization represents 12,000 builders statewide, said: "We're not opposed to good planning, but we aren't in favor of the bill. There are things we can do better, but our policy is if it's not broken, don't fix it."

One person who would probably like to fix *him* is the highly Honorable Judge John "Fastidious" Feikens, a U. S. Circuit judge who, since 1977, has taken on such personages as former Mayor Coleman Young and the less descript officials throughout the suburbs of Detroit, and won. First, the judge forced Detroit to make over a billion dollars worth of improvements in its sewage treatment plant. Then, he held the prospect of hefty fines over St. Clair Shores, Clinton Township, Mt. Clemens, and other violators, who have admitted to dumping hundreds of billions of gallons of raw sewage directly into Lake St. Clair. Feikens set these miscreants to digging up their pavements and expanding their sewage treatment capacity. Furthermore, this Phantom of the Judiciary put the entire region on notice that if further developments occurred without adequately addressing the waste disposal problem, he would put a hold on building permits everywhere (including Hell); huge fines; and find other forms of chastisement suitable to the gutter-tumbling behavior of various locales.

Classic Gutter-Tumbling

Lakefront owners and sun-loving sons of guns, in particular, are in a dither over the fact that Canadian geese, ducks, and other such apparent enemies of nature have been impudently dropping their homage on beaches; this homage then washes into the waters and inculcates E Coli bacteria and other skin defoliants. Of course, it should be pointed out that as open fields, woodlands, and marshes are paved and eliminated, the State of Michigan has neglected to install rest areas for feather bearing life-forms near its beyond-ample highway system.

Meanwhile a bird of another feather, Governor John "The Egret" Engler, inadvertantly enlightened us about the major problems of finessing our flushage. On 10 July, Engler was quoted in George Weeks' column in the Detroit *News* as saying, "It doesn't matter, seemingly, what the field is, including industry and local politics. Look how difficult it is to get people to run for school board or city council seats."

What seems to have happened, if the City of Warren is the paradigm, is that this vacuum on city councils, mayoralties, zoning boards, and township planning boards was filled largely by real estate development moguls or by their cronies. This may help to explain the problems of runaway sprawl more than anyone may suspect!

On 16 June 1999, the Detroit *Free Press* reported how a luxury home development, built by a Warren planning commissioner (!), had sewer lines put in without inspection and without the requisite permits in that city. The sewers feed into Red Run drain and, ultimately, Lake St. Clair. The State Department of Environmental Quality issued a $19,000 fine to the *City of Warren* when it was discovered that the lines were put in at the Chicago Road Estates, a development in which some Warren City Council members are building homes.

Of course, in 'burb after 'burb, it is the mayor and city council members who hire and/or approve city inspectors who are supposedly guarding the public trust and waterways. Besides infiltrating small town politics, another tactic that developers use to facilitate sprawl was seen in Washtenaw Township when the planners there refused to rezone farmland for planned subdivisions. The developers, with deep pockets, sued the township. The township, having insufficient funds to fight in court, caved in.

All of the examples above point to the promulgation of negative externalities, i.e. economic spillover costs that affect all of society. Urban, suburban and rural areas must bear these costs in the face of ongoing megapolitan sprawl. The hope for the future rests upon enforcement by a strong and true legal system. Unplanned growth, if left unchecked, will have not only a far-reaching environmental impact, but a far-reaching economic impact as well.

Sure, in the 19th Century, Manifest Destiny despoiled and uprooted Native Americans (and Mexicans), not to mention the buffalo, grizzly bears, and millions of trees and rivers. However, it never ceased, and now has caromed in a vengeful wave that that spreads over all of America and uproots and erodes us this very day. The Indians have their casinos and reservations, which they control. One has to wonder, where will the children of the rest of us go?

Chapter 2

The New Urbanism:
From Chaos to Complexity

"I can't get no respect. My wife complained about our house--said it ain't got no class or no character, and that it looks like every other house in the neighborhood. I says, 'Why not bring your mother over here, we'll stick her face in some wet cement. Then we'll have gargoyles.'"
--Rodney Dangerfield

In the first chapter, we discussed urban sprawl and how it was the logical, if unseen, extension of Manifest Destiny. We referred to some of the legal tactics that developers have evolved in order to call their own shots. Primarily, they either insinuate themselves, or their henchmen, onto city councils, mayoralties, or planning boards, or they scoop up properties and, pitting their well-funded legal resources against the modest wherewithal of townships and country villages, bully their way past local zoning codes. We used the City of Warren to illustrate the first tactic. The second, we said, occurred recently in Washtenaw Township. Now, it is being dramatized in Bloomfield Township at Telegraph and Square Lake Roads.

The Tiebout Hypothesis
In the September, 1998 issue of *Policy Review*, the ultra-conservative publication of the Heritage Foundation, Steven Hayward laid out the battle lines succinctly in an article titled "Legends of the Sprawl." Hayward responded with alarm to the growing popularity of New Urbanism, which is also synonymous with the "Smart Growth" policies of Al Gore. In this article, *Policy Review* brought up "The Tiebout Hypothesis." Hayward said, "University of Chicago economist Charles Tiebout posited in his 1956 article 'A Pure Theory of Local Expenditures' that there is no objective way to determine the 'right' level of public services that a local government should provide. Therefore, the optimal level of local public services is best determined through municipal competition, by which local jurisdictions offer different bundles of public goods and people express their preferences by voting with their feet." Besides sounding like a voting booth in Florida, this "voting with their feet" idea accurately describes

13

the stampede that occurred in most American cities during the 1950s and 60s and which established the suburban way of life in America. The fact that this stampede continued through the 70s, 80s and 90s, and still continues, is problematic. It is, in a word, chaos!

The System as an Organism

Writing in *World Futures*, the journal of the General Evolutions Group, Hu Tao of the Chinese Academy of Sciences stated, "The so-called self-organizing system, just like a lotus out of mud, can organize new structures in its environment, which are more orderly that the environment itself. If a system can only respond passively to environmental stimulation, then it will be organized by its environment and cannot organize itself. So, a self-organizing system must have active action on its environment, i.e. it must have self-creativity--this is the cardinal difference."[9]

Arising out of modern physics, the science of Complexity is a grown-up version of Chaos Theory. Complexity Theory posits that all systems--molecules, ecosystems, economies, and galaxies--subscribe to very common principles of evolution. In the May, 1993 issue of *World Futures*, Geoffrey Hodgson of Cambridge University referred to the self-creativity of systems in an essay titled "The Economy as an Organism--not a Machine." Hodgson wrote, "Recognition of the function of variety in an evolving system leads to a toleration of a variety of structure and ownership.... Variety and impurity are essential to test all structures and systems on a pragmatic, experimental, and evolutionary basis." What seldom occurs to most of us, caught as we are in the stampede of chaos, is that we are the economy. We are the system! The New Urbanism--or "Smart Growth" Movement--is a disparate tendency, an evolutionary testing by the system toward self-creativity. Every component of the system is interconnected. There is legal testing; political and philosophical testing; environmental, architectural, and market testing. Perhaps some deeper evolutionary laws are prodding the self-organizing tendencies of our society to a more complex level of organization beyond the guiding hands of real estate agents and local politicians.

That might explain the complex interrelationship of policies that defy outmoded labels. While *Policy Review* sneers at the "new liberalism" of New Urbanism, how would these conservatives respond to Governor Engler's Brownfield Development Program, in which the State of Michigan is helping to underwrite the costs of converting polluted tracts in Detroit (and other Michigan cities) into viable plots for redevelopment. "Infill," the economic recycling of urban wastelands and vacant plots, is a major principle of Smart Growth. The concept of "Enterprise Zones," which involves earmarking major tracts of land for development incentives, was the original brainchild of Jack Kemp, Bob Dole's running mate in 1996, and was promoted in Michigan by John Engler. This program established a part of Detroit as an "Enterprise Zone" and has been vastly beneficial.

Another major plank of New Urbanism and a bane to the market fundamentalists at *Policy Review* (and the Detroit *News*) is Regional Governance. Disparate county executives such as Ed McNamara, Brooks Patterson, and John Hertel are tentatively embracing this concept.

Gurus of Growth

As with the lot of evolution, much that occurs is below public consciousness. Complexity thinkers suggest that systems have a sort of Jungian collective unconscious. However, there is a growing emergence and, as *Policy Review* notes with alarm, a growing popularity. For example, with his 1996 book *Metropolitics*, Myron Orfield[10] proved himself to be a leading thinker in the field of urban growth, as did David Rusk in his book *Cities Without Suburbs*.[11] In May of this year, *Newsweek* magazine did a major article on urban growth.

A more esoteric and lovely book is *Ecological Design* by Sim VanderRyn and Stuart Cowan.[12] In this work, the authors put forth three major principles; "everyone is a designer," "design with nature," and "solutions grow with place." As a Complexity thinker, Stuart Cowan suggests, "If we embrace slime molds and duckweed as esteemed teachers and role models, humankind has a chance." With real-life examples and contemplative prose, the authors demonstrate what an ecology-based way of thinking is, and how it can sprout environmentally- and economically-sustainable design solution for systems including place, technologies and organizations.

As urban sprawl puts severe demands on these limited public resources, legal battles over rights will ensue. The central issue is the rights of individual municipalities versus the general welfare of an entire region in the production, delivery, and maintenance of elements of infrastructure. Some municipalities control basic utilities, such as water, as well as regional infrastructures, e.g. streets and parks. Everyone from Judge John "Feisty" Feikens to the Michigan Association of Home Builders, the EPA, and various Michigan mayors are crossing swords. The New Urbanists warn that there needs to be some regional power coalescing in the public sector. Self-creativity: if a system doesn't have it, then this system will be organized by its environment--perhaps to extinction. We need regional power in order to counterbalance the Deep Pockets of vested interests who are using classic divide-and-conquer tactics. If we don't pay attention to some of the "two-serving" politicians on city councils and planning commissions, we may forever blunder about like herd animals without a clue. We have no prediction as to how these legal battles will go (rent the video of *Chinatown* for some suggestions). Therefore, we will end with a question: will the Southeastern Michigan Council of Governments (SEMCOG) have any real power in this matter?

Chapter 3

Reinventing Cities

"Wayne County ranked first in the nation and Michigan fifth in the percent of households in foreclosure. In 2006, according to data released last week by RealtyTrac, one of every 21 Wayne households entered foreclosure last year, the equivalent of 40,219 households."
--Brian O'Conner, "Home Price Slide Not Over," *Detroit News*, 1 February 2007

Prologue
Based upon congressional estimates to September 2009, the cost of the wars in Iraq and Afghanistan has exceeded $1 trillion (costofwar.com). To the average U.S. household of 2.6 persons, this represents $8 thousand less income to spend on housing, cars, food, or clothing. In other words, in Michigan this same amount would have paid the salaries of 4,900 public-school teachers for one year, or would have paid for 2,800 public housing units (ibid, census.gov).

Unreal Estate
A few years ago, as we traveled north on the Lodge freeway from the Auto Show at Cobo Hall, the cab driver showed us one of the more obscure urban curiosities: "Viaducks, I call them, or Freeway Children," the driver said. "You have to look hard, but they are there every night, in the worst cold... whatever. They're territorial. The same ones sleep under the same bridges. Only every month, I see them under more bridges than the month before."

Sure enough, we saw these "Viaducks" again the next night. You may see them easily, too. Head north from Cobo and turn right on northbound I-75. They are there, on the left ledge. The Viaducks are curled up in rags, old blankets, and cardboard. Some have garbage bags full of cans and bottles. Head further north on the Lodge and you will find that four out of five viaducts feature the same nondescript individuals. "Kind of reminds me of New Orleans, but without the water," the driver quipped. A couple of weeks have passed since that trip from the Auto Show. We checked on the Viaducks again, this time in below-zero temperatures. Lo and behold, the Viaducks remain. We remember another thing that the cab driver said about the Viaducks, "Every day, at 7:00 a.m., they line up on Grand River and the Lodge service drive, and vans pick many of them up. They are taken all around the area to deliver handbills. Chances are good they've been to your house."

New Hotels

Just as New Orleans was, we predict that Detroit is going to be a big convention town. Three new hotels soon will come on line. They are associated with the three casinos, as stipulated in the contract agreements that granted the casinos their gaming licenses. Even so, development money has poured into reviving the old Book Cadillac and Pick-Fort Shelby hotels, mammoth, ornate, and formerly opulent structures that have been closed for more than fifteen years. Given that conventions are booked three to five years in advance, it would seem that the smart money has been operating behind the scenes with foreknowledge of the impending increase in market demand.

This activity coincides with a gradual re-gentrification movement in the Cass Corridor--that vast slum south of the Cultural Center and WSU that extends to the edge of the Central Business District. As an aside, let us remark on our disdain for the pseudo-sociological hallucination that infects those who refer to such movements as "gentrification" rather than re-gentrification. This is so because the fascinating architecture that has become haunted grottos of boarded-up petrificants was inhabited originally by the city's middle and upper classes a century ago. However, when the Seville Apartment building at 3170 Second Ave. (on the cusp of what used to be Chinatown) was cleared and leveled in 1999, no less than twelve dead bodies were found. Two of them were newborn babies, presumably abandoned by drug-addled prostitutes. The remainder of the twelve died presumably from either the elements or drug overdoses. The full horror of this subterranean area was documented by P.T. Halley in his article "An Evolutionary View of the Underground Economy."[13]

Abandoned long ago by the Chinese and others who migrated to suburbia, the Cass Corridor became an unofficial red-light district and a center of social-service facilities. The Corridor concentrated homeless shelters, rehab centers, drug dens, cheap motels, and apartment buildings that were permeated by cast-offs, sexual tourists, and the marginally employed. However, after the Salvation Army closed its center on Park at Sproat Street (a gigantic twenty-six story structure that served as a homeless shelter, drug-rehab facility, and halfway house), many of the clients that it served remained in the area. The Viaducks represent the last holdouts of what was once a panoramic mental wilderness. The Viaducks can't leave. Structurally coupled and magnetized by territoriality, they also sleep downtown in bus shelters, doorways, or in the few abandoned structures that haven't yet been converted to lofts or luxury condos. They also frequent the casinos, which are open 24/7, to pass the time, keep warm, or snatch a purse or two.

18

When is a Law Not a Law?

Unlike the laws of gravity, matter, and energy, the laws governing fields such as economics, psychology, and sociology are somewhat provisional and contextual. For example, the laws of supply and demand offer approximations or starting points for empirical validation. However, these laws are often circumvented or modified by monopolies, cartels, or, as we shall see, by complex phenomena in the stock and commodities markets. As one travels throughout Detroit and other metropolitan areas, one is struck by the number of "For Sale" signs. Not withstanding the number of foreclosures and vacancies in Michigan, where some 5,000 people per year are leaving the state for largely economic reasons, one would expect a significant increase in the affordability of housing. However, by and large, this is not so—at least not yet.

A brief tour will show apartment complexes advertising one, two, or three months of free rent (a loss leader) or, as some condo developments are offering, a free high-definition television set. Home builders in some markets-- and this is a nationwide phenomena--are offering "no down payment, no payments for eight months" and similar deals. An acquaintance in Ferndale, trying to sell a house unsuccessfully for a year now, considers adding an addendum to his "For Sale" sign reading "Win a free date with an astronaut." Yet we still are plagued by infomercials advertising real-estate training kits, seminars, DVDs, and the whole enchilada. We especially like the infomercial with the ersatz couple lounging on their yacht telling us how they gave up their humdrum jobs and made $100,000 in three months thanks to some equally ersatz real-estate training course. However, as one financial planner remarked to a caller to his radio show, "If there's so much money in real estate, why is this guy [selling the course] traveling the countryside, sleeping in hotel rooms six nights a week, unloading his kit, when *he* could be sitting on a yacht?" Hmm, I wonder? In their *Wall Street Journal* column "The Property Report," James R. Haggerty and Anjali Athavaley tell us how David Lereah, chief economist of the National Association of Realtors, got a big round of applause at their national convention in New Orleans (of all places) in November 2006. In his prediction, he stated that the membership of the association would decrease by six to eight percent over the next year. Essentially, Lereah implied that a whole bunch of them should get lost![14]

Even so, except for some anecdotal evidence and some insignificant "loss-leader" gimmicks, the price of housing is still unaffordable for an increasing number of people. Looked at another way, a home may be in a customer's price range, but there is a reasonable chance that the costs may exceed the value at any given time. As a result, the unpredictability of the market makes such an investment dubious at this juncture. Both of these problems are due to the increasingly complex nature of the real-estate market. Carrick Mollenkamp of the *WSJ* tells us that the mortgage market in the U.S. is a "complicated web of mutually dependent businesses. Mortgages are frequently bought and sold several times over, and the default risk often lands far from the institution that

19

originated a mortgage. Banks and mortgage brokers size up would-be borrowers and make the loans. These lenders sell many of the loans to mortgage wholesalers, which gather them into pools and flip them to large financial institutions or investment banks. Some of these buyers, including Wall Street investment banks, package the mortgages as securities for sale to investors, a process known as securitization."[15]

These securities are bought by hedge funds, trusts, pension funds, and other institutional investors in a real-estate market estimated in value as some $30 trillion in the U.S. Because of this vast investment pool, foreclosures and other hardship cases barely make a bump in the road of solvency--so far--as mortgage holders wait out market slumps. However, most individual sellers cannot hold out. Not surprisingly, there is a tilting or bias in the market favoring the big players. As a result, prices can remain "artificially" high, indefinitely. To illustrate, a mortgage or similar investment company can scoop up a distressed property or foreclosure at auction. With plenty of capital, these companies know that they can flip the properties to a hedge-fund or other instrument. As a result, the property becomes a kind of "unreal" estate--a security, sold on the Chicago Mercantile Exchange. This is why the idea of good schools, safe neighborhoods, access to shopping, and other amenities may be good selling points to an individual buyer, but the lack of such selling points does not make a significant impact on prices to Chinese, British, or other international investors in the global system of exchanges who make their important decisions based ultimately on quarterly earnings expectations.

In the larger reality, the laws of supply and demand in the real-estate market operate in a somewhat paradoxical manner (similar to that of energy markets), through the influence of swashbuckling magnates who will let entire neighborhoods wither and decay, if only to scoop them up later at a pittance. This is accomplished in the same way that energy companies sit on natural gas reserves until the prices suit the will of their investors and ungodly options. It seems that the laws of supply and demand barely operate in our so-called "free market." However, we offer the following set of suggestions: When the price of gasoline is high, we can cut back a bit on our driving. When we are without medical insurance, we may allow ourselves to bleed a bit more (if we are not too fainthearted) before checking in at the hospital. However, when we are without roofs over our heads, sleeping under a freeway bridge is a bit much. We are left to wonder—has the Lodge been shut down in order to put up drapes and carpeting?

Chapter 4

Reinventing Ourselves

"The mercantile community will have been unusually fortunate if during the period of rising prices it has not made great mistakes. Such a period naturally excites the sanguine and the ardent; they fancy the prosperity they see will last always."
--Walter Bagehot[16]

"Houses are sold 'as is.' When one buyer called to complain about finding a dead possum in a newly purchased house, Teresa Kastanes, who is married to Mr. Barnes' (the realtor) lawyer and helps with the business, recalls responding: 'Listen. I'm throwing in the possum for free."
--"As Home Foreclosures Rise, One Investor Buys Dregs."[17]

Will America Be Foreclosed?

Lost in the increasingly fervent discussion of the real estate crisis is the role of property appraisers. Described by some in the real estate industry as a mysterious cult of squinty eyed, stub-toed connoisseurs of the ersatz, these appraisers pass judgment on the value of what is the most important investment that families ever will make. These state-certified practitioners are tested on building-code lore, real estate math, and a host of other subjects. However, it is somewhat mysterious that few lawmakers have come to question and address sufficiently the potential conflicts of interest inherent in this profession. Many stakeholders, including lending institutions, real estate agents, and mortgage brokers, benefit from higher valuations in the form of fees, as cities and townships enjoy a higher property-tax base. Furthermore, states gain in many ways from higher property values by selling themselves as wholesome locations seeking to attract new businesses and residents.

Like Fred Rogers (Mister Rogers), the assessor is everyone's friend in the neighborhood when values are increasing. However, the same assessor is viewed as a skulking menace when the opposite occurs, which is what is happening now. A mortgage broker we know told us that he likes to rotate appraisers to help them to keep their competitive edge. The quid pro quo is not in kickbacks or bribery, excepting anecdotal instances to which we are not privy. Rather, apparently the quid pro quo is how appraisers are rewarded, merely by the frequency of their utilization in the form of a standard fee. However, there are agents from California, New York, North Carolina, and elsewhere buying Michigan homes in Ferndale, Warren, Southgate, and other locales that were appraised at $150,000 and up for a mere $20,000 or so. These agents are acquiring the homes from financial institutions that are dumping their distressed properties.

Of course, this is a much better arrangement than in some neighborhoods of Detroit, where owners simply abandon homes. What is little understood by people outside of "the hood" (and is hardly admitted by those within it) is the phenomenon of Devil's Night arson. Often, it is an informal process in which Property owners clean out veritable viper's nests where drug dealers or loose-fingered homeless people have ensconced themselves and where schoolchildren may have been assaulted. In some cases, though, squatters actually have improved the area in question by the rudimentary improvements and security that they provide by their presence. Even more, some informal entrepreneurs rehab numerous properties--untitled or informally acquired--and rent them out. (If a landlord gives a person a good enough deal, who is likely to inspect his or her credentials?) Still, this question must be asked in a market on the edge of chaos: what is the planet of origin of professional property appraisers?

The Edge of Chaos
We raise this point merely because few others seem to have questioned the impartiality of appraisers. We recognize that they are not the central problem. The central problem is "irrational exuberance." Add to this the irresponsibility of Wall Street bankers and politicians as well as a free market ideology with its "deregulatory exuberance." The partial collapse of property values is not something that came out of the blue. The *Wall Street Journal* has warned of a housing bubble for several years. There have been recent discussions in Congress about legislation against "predatory lending," that is, the practice of lending institutions throwing higher interest loans at persons with questionable credit histories and without proof of income. In turn, the institutions then pool these loans into securities that are sold in the bond market, particularly to unregulated hedge funds. What seems unethical is that while "predatory lending" was allowed to slide as an ostensible way for low-income buyers to gain equity (which is the justification for not stopping it), why was this problem not addressed two years ago when the new consumer credit/bankruptcy laws were enacted? Why now? It is not only the fault of the thousands of fringe mortgage brokers operating out of cars and dive restaurants. GMAC, the automaker's lending arm, now is being reinforced with $1 billion from its parent company in order to cover its exposure to massive defaults in its subprime loan portfolio. So much for last quarter's profit!

Speaking of chaos, some may consider Sean David Morton, a noted conspiracy theorist and gadfly, to be permanently out to lunch. However, he does offer food for thought with his (preposterous?) claim that we heard him utter on the

Coast to Coast radio talk show: China threatened to call in its markers on the trillion or so dollars in bonds that it holds in the U.S. However, Treasury Secretary Henry M. Paulson hinted that "something bad could happen" to China's oil pipelines coming out of Iran, thus cooling down that idea. Something that is not preposterous is the established fact that the stock market is down 1.97% over worries of defaults in the subprime sector of the mortgage market. As Mark Whitehouse and Sarah Lueck point out in the *Wall Street Journal*,[18] many pension funds have been vested in the hedge-fund sector, as have most mutual funds, to some extent. The ripple effects of the housing market downturn affect such blue chippers as Home Depot, Lowe's, and the many companies that manufacture paint, nails, and shingles. In fact, the whole outhouse is quaking and shaking!

"But We're Practically Next Door to Disneyland!"

In his article in the *Orlando Sentinel*, Jack Snyder gives a vivid illustration of the pitfalls of this irrational exuberance as he details the rise and fall of Aleem N. Hussain's real estate venture.[19] Mr. Hussain's company, which did business under the name of Main Street USA, Inc., was presented to the public as a real estate investment trust (REIT), a common investment instrument used by developers and finance companies. Hussain's 300 or so investors in Orlando each face potential losses of up to $400,000. These include many who used their entire life savings or who took out loans to get into what didn't start out to be but wound up as a pyramid scam like Enron.

Starting in a booming market, Mr. Hussain bought Waldengreen Apartments in southwest Orlando, a complex that he began to convert into condos. In the market, timing is everything. However, in the time that it took for Hussain to gather the investors, purchase the complex, hire the construction people, and market the property, the demand for condos started to sag like the bossom of Florida matron Magda in the film *There's Something about Mary*[20]. Hussain "sold" the first few condos that he completed to relatives as a way to convince the appraisers of the "true" market value of these condos. He held investment seminars at the community center and hired the community-relations director of the Orlando County Sheriff's Office to tout his scheme at these gatherings. However, Hussain never achieved the critical mass of organization, finance, and market timing to complete the project before it became apparent that valuations were reversing course. Market saturation had set in.

Snyder reports that R. Scott Shuker, a lawyer representing Main Street USA and two subsidiaries in the Chapter 11 bankruptcy filing, "recently told a bankruptcy judge in Orlando that no REIT was ever set up legally and the money was not protected by the FDIC.... Shuker told the bankruptcy court that as much as $10 million could be involved. Snyder finishes by noting, "Creditors are lining up in bankruptcy court to levy claims against those assets, which are heavily mortgaged." In his article in the *Wall Street Journal*,[21] Alex Frangos notes, "Mr. Hussain's rise and fall illustrates one of the hazards of a frothy property market:

inexperienced developers get in over their heads and drag down unsophisticated investors down with them. 'Schoolteachers, cops, doctors, priests, everyone thought they were Donald Trump,' says Lewis Freeman, the court-appointed trustee administering Main Street's bankruptcy proceeding. Mr. Hussain's company, he contends, was a 'microcosm of the total market. You had a lot of unqualified people getting easy money and able to go into businesses in which they didn't know what they were doing.'"

An X-Ray of the Invisible Hand

With better timing and perhaps with the help of a consultant, Hussain might have succeeded. If he was ambitious, Hussain then would have been positioned to approach Wells Fargo, Goldman Sachs, or J.P. Morgan about a collateralized debt obligation (CDO). Serena Ng and Michael Hudson of the *WSJ* explain that a CDO is the investment instrument that "has acted like a locomotive in the housing-finance business, driving growth by soaking up risky mortgage bonds and parceling them out to investors around the world."[22] CDOs are an integral part of Wall Street's mortgage slicing-and-dicing machine. After mortgages are written, investment banks pool them together and use the cash flows produced by them to pay off mortgage-backed bonds that the investment banks underwrite.

Ng and Hudson say that the mortgage bonds "are often packaged again into CDOs and sold off in slices. Investors can choose to buy the risky pieces of the bonds or purchase slices with less risk. Last year, CDOs soaked up an estimated $150 billion of mortgage-backed bonds, the vast majority of which were underpinned by subprime mortgages." What happened was that investors, betting on home appreciation, scooped up these bonds avidly because subprime mortgages have higher interest rates (12% as opposed to the average 6% for prime mortgages.) Home buyers also gambled on rising appraisals, buying into adjustable rate mortgages (ARMs) that start with low interest but then balloon after a few years. Of course, some home buyers bought into the infamous interest-only loans, with low or no down payments, betting that rising equity would, well, give them equity. Depending on when they bought, it did or did not—one more factor feeding the growing spread of mortgage defaults in the U.S. this year.

All in all, practices from many camps from within the housing and lending industries have caused the issues connected to real estate affordability and mortgage default. As the examples above demonstrate, these problems have tangled together like a bunch of yarn, leaving the legal community to undo the knots. Swift action by the congressional committees investigating these issues as well as aggressive diligence through the judiciary process may be the only ways to reverse this calamity.

Chapter 5

We Are the City

"'I remember like it was yesterday—to hell with it, Wal-Mart will buy the whole damn town, we'll shut them down! We used to drive through towns,' he points in succession at imaginary stores, 'We'd say six months, three months, six months. Which one of you will be closing next.'"
--Welden Nicholson, former trainer of store managers at Wal-Mart[23]

Wal-Mart: The Retail Smile of Wholesale Misery

Filmmaker Robert Greenwald spent nine months semi-undercover creating an explosive documentary titled *Wal-Mart: The High Cost of Low Price*. He intended it to be a scathing indictment of the retail giant. Perhaps inadvertently, this film-- and most of the Wal-Mart critiques that we've seen--describes the culmination of an epoch in the same way that a cyst may reveal some cellular malady more profound than its scabrous fulmination.

As the world's largest retailer, with annual revenues of $256 billion from more than 5,100 stores, Wal-Mart—like the U.S.—is the big kid on the block. It sticks out like a sore thumb in the known universe. As such, Wal-Mart is at the epicenter of mass dislocations in the global economy—the grinning skull behind the face of a new beast. It is not the cause of this phenomenon, but rather the flag-bearer of a conquering army whose soldiers are stockholders with a mercenary's allegiance that is always up for grabs. Wal-Mart has refined and systematized many of the egregious practices of a whole generation, practices that have endured or have helped to create the paradigm shift in America from stakeholder to shareholder capitalism. As we critique the Wal-Mart institution via this film, we are aware that the scathing finger that we point actually points both ways. Happy shopping, y'all!

Panic in Aisle Five

Greenwald delivers a deservedly ugly portrayal of a corporation in the Michael Moore style, albeit in a rather poetic and effective manner. However, it would have been better for him to have included interviews with some economists to contextualize his critique. This is the primary weakness of all of the Wal-Mart

25

rebukes that we have viewed or read. Yes, $8.00 per hour is no longer a living wage. However, should one of these stores be ensconced within the City of Detroit and put up "Help-Wanted" signs, there would probably be 3,000 or more applicants lining up hours before the office opens, as happened with K-Mart some years ago. The film reveals how Wal-Mart personnel managers help to steer their employees to Social Service offices to apply for Section 8 housing, food stamps, and Medicaid. However, this merely belabors the obvious: that the United States is imploding economically on many fronts. A few years from now, when their buy-out packages are spent, ask released autoworkers if their union leaders have given similar advice. If not, ask this question: should they be rebuked?

As economists, we would elaborate on Greenwald's points in the context of corporate welfare. At least it is consistent that Wal-Mart steers its employees to welfare, given the largesse that it has received in its drive to retail domination. In the union-financed screed *Shopping for Subsidies: How Wal-Mart Uses Taxpayer Money to Finance Its Never-Ending Growth*,[24] Jeff McCourt documents that various government subsidies to finance the expansion of Wal-Mart totaled some $624 million for only 91 stores. That is an average of $6.9 million per store.

We would add this. When a business sets up in a new location, there always are infrastructure costs for sewer lines, utilities, roads, and increased protection from crime and fire. During the economic recessions of the 1970s, and particularly in relation to the "energy crisis" due to the OPEC oil embargo, various industries have shopped their inestimable presence to various localities in a manner resembling an auction. Thus, Governor Granholm's duties (with the help of actor Jeff Daniels in television commercials promoting Michigan's business climate) include luring job-creating businesses to Michigan for the good of the commonweal. In the 1970s, Detroit proper lost some 250,000 auto and auto-related jobs to far-flung townships, a variety of other states, and offshore locations. Previously nondescript places in Michigan such as Lake Orion or Tecumseh and locals in Indiana and Tennessee would offer free land, tax abatements, free infrastructure additions or, in some cases, "right-to-work" laws that favor non-union enterprises. They successfully attracted GM, Ford, Daimler-Chrysler, and Toyota, which established plants. This pattern has been duplicated by industries across the economic spectrum and now is taught in leading MBA programs. (In fairness, we should note that GM, Ford, and Daimler-Chrysler have experienced large decreases in domestic market share during this entire time to the point that, if these three were to merge together, then their combined domestic automobile market share would only be 55%-- arguably below the market-share limit held in antitrust case law.)

However, this is a positive-sum game. Over time, this industry adds to local tax bases, resulting in the birth--or rebirth--of entire communities. As Greenwald illuminates rightfully, Wal-Mart has exploited this opportunity to the chagrin of local taxpayers and members of Chambers of Commerce. Wal-Mart has moved into towns with promises of new jobs and future tax revenues. However, when tax abatements expire, Wal-Mart closes shop. In some instances, it has opened new stores just outside of the town limits, thus avoiding a day of reckoning. This zero-sum game results in the wholesale destruction of local businesses that previously have paid taxes and provided employment. What results is a loss of jobs by those local businesses that usually paid better than Wal-Mart. Also, there is the blight of empty Wal-Mart stores, which take up hundreds of acres of what used to be either farmland or small-town mom-and-pop establishments. The film presents poignant scenes of countless boarded-up storefronts and abandoned parking spaces while Bruce Springsteen performs a touching rendition of Woody Guthrie's "This Land is Your Land." Today, Mayberry is looking like New Orleans sans water!

This Land IS Your Land
Of course, Target, K-Mart, Sears, et al previously have established the practices that Wal-Mart has systematized and refined to a cunning form. However, these other giant retailers stick to the agreements that they make with the towns involved. When one of these retailers moves out, some other franchise usually moves to take its place. Regarding this point, Greenwald is weak. He implies that Wal-Mart is an invader from Mars. However, he neglects to mention that there already are established aliens from Venus, Neptune, and other points hither and yon. In addition, Wal-Mart also has been hit with fines for employing undocumented aliens (non-U.S. citizens). However, when one can wander into a K-Mart store at three o'clock in the morning and hear nothing but Spanish from the sweepers and moppers, one must wonder.

In Greenwald's film, a housekeeper with an Eastern European accent complains of being locked in her Wal-Mart store until dawn and being shorted on the wages that she should have received. In fact, Wal-Mart already has paid $50 million in a class-action suit in Colorado. In a pending suit in Texas, it has been alleged that the chain has cheated employees of $150 million. The film features several former managers and a trainer of managers who illustrate various techniques that they employed to pressure workers into working unpaid overtime—methods that are being studied by other retail giants even now. Of course, some of us can remember when Sears began to hire only part-time workers in the 1980s in an effort to avoid pension, health insurance, and other benefits. As we have stated, as strong an indictment as Greenwald makes in this weeper, we wish that he would have had a labor or urban economist explain that most of these practices are a pattern that began with the epochal shift in America from shareholder to stakeholder capitalism. This shift was engendered by Reagan-era tax cuts on capital gains and policies that favored a weakening of Anti-Trust enforcement. This represents a "New Federalism" theory that ostensibly shifted power to the States. This meant an end to Federal aid to large cities and the act of state governments auctioning against each other for whatever industrial or commercial expansion may have occurred. Finally, it created grant-allocation policies that argued against regional or local planning.

Indeed, it would take more than one film or book to document this shift, which has occurred not merely due to an ideological revolution, though deliberate policies associated with supply-side economics and the "Reagan Revolution" played significant parts in the drama. The fact is that the United States had exalted, historic advantages after World War II due to the collapse of our global competitors—their infrastructure, markets, and currencies. These advantages came to an end by the 1970s when our corporations found that global competition had returned with a vengeance.

Are we in a new era? Using a rolling scroll, Greenwald lists towns and cities that have rejected Wal-Mart's overtures. Scores of cities, including Charlevoix and Livonia in Michigan, have rejected this predatory business model. According to David Wessel of the *Wall Street Journal*,[25] Charles Rangel (D-NY), the new chairman of the House Ways and Means Committee, is "expected to complicate the White House's efforts to further liberalize trade by demanding strong protections for labor in any trade talks." Wessel also predicts that Democrats probably will negate the President's "fast-track" authority on trade deals this year. Wessel concludes, "Leo Gerard, president of the United Steelworkers Union, told reporters yesterday that the coming showdown is but 'the first battle we're going to win.'"

Indeed, Wal-Mart has been thwarted this year in its bid to secure a regulatory blessing to open banks in its stores. It has halted plans for any further expansions as a matter of policy. Further installments in this series will examine similar issues of sprawl, re-gentrification, and other aspects of what may be a growing movement loosely called "New Urbanism."

Chapter 6

We Are the City, Constantly Reinvented

"Eye-popping bribes in the range of $10,000 to $30,000 per promised job in the 80s now seem modest. Alabama, South Carolina, Michigan, and Mississippi spent $59,000 to $193,000 per job to attract or retain various auto plants in the 1990s."

--Michael Shuman, *The Small-Mart Revolution* (Berrett-Koehler Publishers, 2006)

This Is Not Mayberry!

As they say, the future is not what it used to be. If the past election indicates anything besides distaste for the war in Iraq, it also reflects revulsion toward and potential correction of the combination of forces loosely called "globalization," with its attendant job insecurities. In addition, we could add that globalization has led to a corroded tax base in Michigan and to the freefall of home values--and we are not even in a recession! To add insult to injury, even the bullets that criminals fire at citizens are made in China. (This detracts from what possibly could have been a promising growth industry.)

The questions seem to be: Will people, bought out by cheap consumer products and dubious promises of "retraining," continue to suffer endless economic dislocations with passivity? Will people hold their feet to the fire of politicians like Congressman John Dingell who soon will head the important Commerce Committee in Congress? On *Meet the Press*, Dingell asserted recently that he will fight for a reversal of the tax benefits that companies get for relocating overseas. He also said that he would work on forcing currency manipulations of our Asian competitors, via tariffs.

A few years ago, we heard of a snarl in Oak Park. According to Julie Edgar in her column in the *Detroit Free Press*,[26] the city is suing ASC Inc. for $110,000 in lost tax revenue that the company received as an abatement in 2000, in a contract that was to last until 2008. Like so many companies have done, ASC allegedly went fishing for locations, in the sort of subsidy auction that Wal-Mart has made famous, only to relocate just before the time of reckoning. Oak Park city manager Jim Hock said, "We shouldn't be competing with Berkley or Royal

Oak for a business to relocate a mile away and leave abandoned buildings so they can get a fifty-percent tax abatement." Apparently, as Mr. Hock indicated, ASC is moving from Berkley at Eleven Mile Road east of Greenfield to the City of Southfield (though the article stated incorrectly that it is moving to Southgate).

If this were Mayberry, we could depend on Sheriff Andy Taylor to give them boys at ASC a little talking to. However, this is not Mayberry, and there are plenty of attorneys in the area with things to say about the ASC matter. This brings us to an editorial in the *Wall Street Journal*[27] that huffed and puffed as it attacked a class-action lawsuit launched against Wal-Mart in San Francisco. The editors stated, "Commonality is supposed to be the essence of class actions, yet the vast majority of Wal-Mart employment decisions are discretionary and made by individuals at thousands of locations across the country. But never mind. The San Francisco court said plaintiffs' statistics could justify class treatment and certified the largest private civil rights case in history."

The lawsuit contends that there is a systematic bias in the pay and promotion of women, as documented in *Wal-Mart, The High Cost of Low Price*,[28] the film that we reviewed in preceding chapter. The documentary also suggests that this is just the beginning of civil action; other large lawsuits could well be on the way. The *WSJ* editorial suggests that what the newspaper and its corporate clients seem to fear most is that a class action precludes the most obvious legal tactic of divide and conquer. They know that potential plaintiffs, cowed already by the world's largest corporation, with its legion of first-rate attorneys, and clinging to a precarious economic position, surely would be less likely to step up individually and risk what little security they have over a potential gain. It is the implications of this plantation mentality that should make this case one of particular interest.

The Small-Mart Revolution

Michael H. Shuman's book *The Small-Mart Revolution: How Local Businesses Are Beating the Global Competition*[29], has a dust jacket that features a photograph of a weathered-looking man of advancing years who is wearing a baseball cap and apron. He looks like he just got his hair cut at Floyd's Barbershop in little ol' Mayberry. This gentleman is standing outside his old-fashioned hardware store--arms crossed, and ready for business. The determination in the face of fear reflected in his countenance shows the veracity of his situation. Like the truth of this man's experience, there is much truth to Shuman's analyses, even if some of his recommended solutions may prove impractical.

Shuman asserts in his introduction, "There is a capitalist alternative gaining acceptance across the United States and throughout the world: economic development rooted in Local Ownership and Import Substitution, or LOIS for short." The idea of local ownership posits not only the nostalgic feel of an old-fashioned downtown but also the economic worth to a community. This is done by increasing the multiplier effect of dollars spent locally by constantly recycling them within a given parameter. As a tacit antidote to the evisceration suffered locally by the onslaught of globalism, Shuman proposes a consciously and systematically employed movement of consumers and producers to decentralize power economically and politically. He wants us to invest in local banks, stores, and other businesses and use all of our civic powers to reject multinationalism and absentee capitalism. In short, he offers not just an idea, but systematic plans and proposals in detail--quite grandiose and transformative, but unlikely to return us to Mayberry.

We would like to mention Korie Wilkins' article in the *Detroit Free Press*,[30] which is about the resurrection of an urban legend (or eyesore)--the former Northville Psychiatric Hospital. Abandoned for almost a generation, this 415-acre site long has been the haunt of adventurous youth, who wander and marvel in dark surrealist revel. Informally, the hospital has been a theme park. However, a draft has been approved by township planners and awaits formal approval. The grounds are to be converted to a development that, according to Wilkins, will include, "1,000 houses parks, senior housing, a downtown-like area of restaurants, stores, offices and entertainment sites, walking trails and possibly an elementary school." (Moving the tombstones but not the graves?) This kind of locally tailored development, one that it is locally planned and approved, is the type that Shuman advocates in his book. In fact, many small communities like Northville, Plymouth, Royal Oak, Ferndale, and Berkley are working hard to preserve the locally-owned businesses and small-town orientation that not only feels but acts like an actual community.

The Devil Is Not in the Details
'Tis folly, as Shuman documents, that Governor Pataki of New York recently gave IBM $500,000 per job as an inducement not to move out of the state. Shuman also tells us that "Governor Bush of Florida dispensed $1,000,000 per job to attract the Scripps Biological Research Center, and Governor Gary Locke of Washington paid a whopping $2,500,000 per job to prevent Boeing from removing the remnants of its operations in the state (Boeing management already fled to Chicago). The anecdotal evidence suggests that the bidding wars for TINA businesses are actually escalating." Shuman introduces the concept of TINA, an acronym for "There Is No Alternative," which implies that global corporations are fishing communities for auctions of land, tax abatements, grants, regulatory relief, and what the author calls a "favorable investment climate." It goes without saying that this also includes Tort Reform of some variety.

We cannot help but remark that the "great" welfare reform done during the Clinton administration as an extension of the Republican "Contract with America" that occurred during a time of robust growth and budget surpluses. Even as far back as the early 1970s, Richard Nixon and others supported a guaranteed annual income for every American. It would seem that the best way to get people to support their local economies would be to make sure that they have at least some money. However as Shuman demonstrates, there is plenty of welfare money going the other way.

Does all of this help to explain why lawyers and bartenders--some of the few remaining partisans of locally-owned and functioning establishments--are perhaps each other's best customers? Until the day that there are drive-through liquor joints and Attorneys R Us franchises, we admit that there is some hope on both sides of the bar. Seriously though, while many of Shuman's proposals and the ideas of local and regional planning are beginning to be taken seriously, an exhaustive look at this indicates the need for a complete and laborious transformation of the American countryside that would involve tremendous commitment and a utopian resolve that may be too demanding for our average couch potato. However, we believe that they are useful for planners, city council members, mayors, and economics professors. On the other hand, it may take a severe recession or a total collapse of the global economy to bring these concepts to fruition. In the meantime, the most useful measures to deal with what Shuman calls "massive economic dislocation" or what we can call YAGS (You Are Getting Screwed) would be national policies. These would include a revival of antitrust enforcement, revision or scrapping of trade treaties, and selective attention to tariffs. In addition, it would prove useful to revise the tax code to favor local investment and discourage its opposite. Furthermore, it would be wise to revisit the various tort reforms to make class-actions and other public-interest causes more achievable.

Chapter 7

Reinventing Cities, Reinventing Ourselves

"The House Appropriations Subcommittee on Military Quality of Life and Veterans Affairs heard testimony last year regarding predatory lenders outside the gates of military bases who target young service members in need of short-term cash and who are unaware of the potentially ruinous terms of loans, which may carry interest rates of up to 2,000%."
--Joseph L. Barnes, National Executive Secretary, Fleet Reserve Association[31]

Easy Money and Creative Destruction

Apart from Milton Freedman, perhaps no economic philosopher has had more impact on Conservative economic thought than Joseph Schumpeter. His principle of "Creative Destruction" has been a mantra used to support everything from globalism and the carnage that it has reaped on domestic manufacturing to deregulation and other aspects of unbridled competition. The idea is that unimpeded market forces are the purest arbiters of social welfare. The philosophy of Creative Destruction also contends that we can solve our problems through unhindered growth, with new products, fresh competitive techniques, and innovative technology. For example, the pain suffered by owners of horse-drawn carriages is but a minor blip in comparison to the gains engendered by the automobile. The latest homage to Schumpeter appears in *Prophet of Innovation*,[32] a book by Thomas McGraw that was reviewed recently by Dan Seligman in the *Wall Street Journal*.[33] Seligman lauds Schumpeter for his recognition (or elevation, depending upon how you look at it) of the entrepreneur as the mythic hero of social economic change. The sometimes ruthless power-seeking of the entrepreneur raises everyone's standard of living. Interestingly, Schumpeter failed miserably in the business world but raised his own standard of living by making his fortune as a writer, teacher, and lecturer. Nevertheless, the entrepreneur is everything. We mortals just need to get out of his/her way.

The concept of entrepreneur as mythic hero is, of course, an ideal. The so-called "free market" never really existed except as a notion that has been advanced by lobbyists, subsidized think tanks, and like-minded pundits. One needs only to look at the situation in Iraq to see that Chaotic Destruction is sometimes the practical result of the imposition of idealism upon complex historical realities. Innovation, seen as an unqualified good, was reconsidered by the Nobel brothers, the inventors of dynamite, who established a "Peace Prize" as partial atonement for the riches that they acquired from their patent.

As for cities, we only need to look at the ravages of sprawl--the phenomena that "there's no there, there"--to see a longing for place and community. In her article "Reinventing the Downtown,"[34] Christina Stolarz reported that the town of Fraser, Michigan will join Novi, Farmington Hills, and other suburban communities in an attempt to establish gravitas by building small stores, non-chain restaurants, and other sentimental edifices. We would guess that a similar sentiment prevails among the dozen or so people who already pledged over a million dollars each to snag a townhouse atop the Book Cadillac Hotel, that arcane, ornamented temple of early 20th Century excess that had been abandoned for fifteen years but is now being renovated. Without dabbling in pop psychology, we offer that, apart from rampant acquisitiveness of larger or newer toys, we hunger for stability and for soul and that this hunger is becoming increasingly visible in our society.

Creative Financial Destruction

Economist Tom Hartman is both the author of three books and the host of a late-night talk show on Air America. On a recent program, he referred to the collapse of the subprime housing market as a classic "bait and switch," whereby a "teaser rate" of 3.5 % interest induces buyers to enter into an adjustable rate mortgage (ARM) that kicks in at 11 % after three years. The idea put forward is that, since housing has been inflating rapidly, the borrower can refinance to a lower fixed-rate mortgage after three years, using the newly acquired equity as collateral.

Since the early 1990s, there has been a fundamental change in banking. In part, this stemmed from legislation that was enacted as a response to the Savings and Loan crisis of the 1980s. This crisis cost the U.S. taxpayers some $500 billion (though some economists claim that the cost has been understated.) Mortgage lenders now earn most of their income from upfront fees rather than from ongoing mortgage interest payments. Mortgage lenders sell their portfolios of mortgages as securities to the investment community. The lenders earn upfront fees both from the original purchase of homes and from their refinancing. In selling off the mortgages, lenders gain from their split of the interest premium—the gap between what the mortgage is worth to the home-buyer and what the same mortgage is worth to the securities investor.

To complicate matters further, there are now roving bands of investors--usually cloaked by real estate trusts (RETs)—who are scooping up homes that were once appraised at $150,000 or more for $20,000 or $30,000. These investors acquire the homes in question from those financial intermediaries that foreclosed on thousands of Detroiters. Allegedly, these marauders have an "in" with these financial institutions, which also earn revenue from the upfront fees that they receive from these transactions. The actual losses accrue to the hedge funds or to whoever bought these securities. These funds often are administrated through the same institutions, at a fee, of course. Hopefully, Senator Carl M. Levin (D-MI), chair of the Senate Permanent Subcommittee on Investigations, and Senator Christopher J. Dodd (D-CT) chair of the Senate Banking Committee, will include these entities and their practices in their investigations.

According to Andy Laperriere of the International Strategy & Investment Group,[35] it is not just working-class stiffs who have gone into default: "Far from being limited to the subprime market, the data show these risky loan features have become widespread. According to Credit Suisse [the Swiss bank], the number of no or low documentation loans--so-called 'liar loans'--has increased to 49% from 18% of purchase loans in 2001, a nearly three-fold increase." Furthermore, the Mortgage Bankers Association of America responded to a recent report issued by the Congressional Joint Economic Committee that shook up investors.[36] The report stated, "We agree that a major cause of foreclosures is local economic conditions, not the fact that loans were made to subprime borrowers. For example, the states of Ohio, Michigan, Indiana, Illinois, and Wisconsin represent only about 14% of outstanding mortgages in the country but account for 28% of the loans in foreclosure, and subprime borrowers account for only about half of the loans in foreclosure in these states."

What this means is that, like the high-tech bubble of the late 1990s, the housing bubble has burst. In a research note published on 9 April 2007, David A Rosenberg, an economist at Merrill Lynch & Co. Inc.,[37] stated that he expects prices to decline 5% next year. He noted "Prices have already flattened over the past twelve months, and, if anything, the inventory situation has deteriorated to record levels.... The backlog of unsold new and existing single-family homes and condominium units for sale has grown 37% in the past year, to 4.4 million."

However, Laperriere and others in the popular press report that home prices could drop as much as 10% this year. A drop of this magnitude could lead to a vicious cycle in the housing market where there will be greater urgency to sell "while the getting is good," and a lesser urgency to buy, e.g. "Let's wait and see how much more it will drop." Laperriere adds that "asset bubbles are harmful for the same reason high inflation is: Both create misleading price signals that lead to a misallocation of economic resources and sow the seeds for an inevitable bust. The unwinding of today's housing bubble is not merely an academic question; it is likely to inflict real hardship on millions of Americans." All bubbles have a common structure--a market distortion in which a huge gap appears in the price to earnings ratio or more complex financial reasons. In other words, you can put lipstick and a nice dress on a pig and take it to the opera. However, ultimately it is still a pig.

35

"And Don't Pass Go"

Alex Pollock, resident fellow of the American Enterprise Institute[38] and author of *The Sarbanes-Oxley Debacle*,[39] presents the Conservative side of this issue. Pollock tells us that the last thing that the mortgage industry needs is another Sarbanes-Oxley Act (originally enacted in response to the high-tech collapse of 2000). It is amazing that people still try to pretend that housing, or any other of the public-traded industries such as oil or health care, represent some free-market ideal. However, if "big government" did not subsidize mortgages by making interest payments tax deductible in addition to offering various subsidized mortgage programs to home-buyers, there wouldn't be much of a mortgage industry. Being in a lower tax bracket, the working-class people in the subprime category benefit less from this subsidy, if at all. As we stated previously, many of us believe that certain interests pushed through the punitive (to consumers) bankruptcy reform law, knowing that such a catastrophe was on the way. For them, Creative Destruction is a boon. Churn is the name of their game: just keep churning the market over and upside down, shake it up, and rake in the fees.

According to the Associated Press release of 5 April 2007, presidential candidate John Edwards said that he wants legislation to help stop high-interest predatory lending. His plan would include matching what low-income Americans are able to save in what he calls individual development accounts, regulating fees that lenders can charge, and, most significantly, as Edwards states, "letting people who declare bankruptcy in falling housing markets cut their mortgage to the current market value."

Almost certainly, the people who live in blighted, rundown neighborhoods are renters, not owners. A real "ownership society" would make more nest eggs for people and less buzzard eggs for predators. These problems in the area of real-estate finance are only part of a set of larger issues. However, they are ones that need to be addressed if we are to hope for (to quote John F. Kennedy) "a rising tide to lift all ships."

Chapter 8

The Real-Estate Market:
Bubble, Bubble, Toil, and Trouble

"According to Yale University economist Robert Shiller, inflation-and quality-adjusted home prices are still more than 50% higher than their averages throughout most of the 20th century. These data suggest that the real-estate correction could have much further to go. Measured savings rates in the U.S. are essentially zero, and the trade deficit is running at 7% of GDP."
--Burton Malkiel, *A Random Walk Down Wall Street*[40]

There are many startling similarities between the high-tech bubble that began to collapse in 2000 and the recent real-estate bubble, which now has collapsed in the residential sector and is expected to do the same in the commercial sector by the end of the decade. One of the most startling similarities is the state of irrational exuberance that existed until recently. At the end of the 1990s, there were frenetic leaps in high-tech stocks. Consequently, the stampede of investors entering the market (urged on by morally debauched analysts who urged "buys" on stock issued by banks that these analysts represented or by banks with outstanding loans to the companies that were lauded by these oracles of riches) was a sure sign of a bubble in trouble. In fact, we could call all of these "sly deeds of dubious legality." The same course of events is happening in the real-estate market. Therefore, we are experiencing the end of irrational exuberance in this market.

Until recently, one-hundred grand only could get you an outhouse on an ocean front. However, you still would have needed to bring your own toilet paper. In Florida, all that it would take for a realtor to sell a house would be to wait for it to land after the hurricane died down and for some wretch to limp up to the table (Soured grapes–my father purchased some ocean-front property in Florida in the 1920s, only to have it lay under twelve feet of ocean since the Category-Five Hurricane of 1928.) However, real estate rose and rose throughout the country, fueled by gullible Trump wannabees who were fired up by get-rich-quick-in-real-estate seminars and made credible by self-dealing appraisers whose thumbs always were up.

That was then, and this is now. Our real-estate market is in a bubble that is bursting, and there is no Glinda the Good Witch to wave her magic wand and say, "Toto, too."

Le Mortgage Macabre

Really now, J.P. Morgan Chase, Wells Fargo, Citigroup, and Deutche Bank all sound like names that we heard mentioned in the Senate and Congressional hearings on the Enron caper.[41] On 3 November 2006, the Hispanic PR Wire posted "LAT Money Center Introduces Nationwide Program That Offers Mortgage Financing to Undocumented Workers."[42] This article states, "LAT Money Centers, a Hispanic-owned financial services company, has introduced the industry's first nationwide financing program for undocumented workers that want to buy homes. This lending program will offer loans to potential homeowners using Individual Taxpayer Identification Numbers (ITIN) and Matricula Consular IDs in lieu of social security numbers." Though recent industry research has shown that Hispanics are less likely to miss payments or to default on their mortgages, one must wonder whether or not these mortgages are being packaged for and marketed to illegal aliens. Timothy Sandos, president of the National Association of Hispanic Real-Estate Professionals,[43] says, "Whoever hits the street first with these loans will be the winner… [a]t least $85 billion of mortgages could be originated from 375,000 households occupied by undocumented renters, up from an estimated $44 billion from 216,000 households a few years ago." A cynical person might suggest that this possibly could explain the political support that exists in some quarters for a "guest-worker program" or further amnesty for undocumented residents. One of the hazards of such a program is that it may result in a move of desperation by mortgage banks and other deed holders of foreclosed properties to sell the properties "temporarily;" to collect the fees, closing costs, etc.; and to dump the mortgages on the bond market, where many of the same or associated financial intermediaries operate. As there is evidence that Hispanic communities, like that in Southwest Detroit, tend prosper in a concentrated space, the bond market could be used to consolidate the mortgages of undocumented residents, to parcel properties further, and to foreclose en masse when the political winds change and the same undocumented residents find themselves the target of deportation. This scenario sounds even more nefarious than that of using dead people to parcel property in the Ventura County dirty-land deal portrayed in the Jack Nicholson film *Chinatown*.[44] Also, it is not too different than the state-sanctioned program used to remove Tevye and his townsfolk in the musical *Fiddler on the Roof*.[45]

According to the myriad of press releases on the subject of mortgages for the undocumented, the banks are accepting government-issued tax-identification numbers for loan applications from illegal immigrants, as they do not have

Social Security numbers. To meet "know-your-customer" requirements, banks often require such borrowers to open a bank account before they approve the loan. Rather than relying on credit history, which may not exist for people living below the radar who often use cash for their purchases, banks pay attention more closely to employment history. However, Sheriff Joe Arpio of Maricopa County, Arizona, whose office has arrested hundreds of illegal immigrants, believes that these banks are taking on a risky proposition.[46] Arpio says that, if he catches these people, then they are going back to Mexico. Consequently, the banks will have a tough time collecting on their loans.

Pump and Dump

Before the posse starts scouring freeway ramps for beggars in brogues and Armani suits, they might consider the facts that that these mortgages are packaged in New York investment houses as securities (mostly bonds) and are sold in bundles mixed with prime mortgages, municipal bonds, and other instruments. This cushions the effects of defaults. Since most of these instruments are scooped up by hedge funds, which generally are considered to be high-risk/high return investment vehicles, the damage to Joe Sixpack as investor is minimized. However, it should be noted that most mutual funds and 401k accounts have some exposure to hedge funds and bonds as diversification strategies and that bond-rating agencies like Moody's and Standard & Poors do a modicum of oversight. Furthermore, hedge funds only are regulated minimally by the SEC. The arcane operation of the funds and the formation of complex derivatives are intelligible to only a small cadre of investors, economists, and the most adept necromancers and cult figures, such as the former CFO of Enron, Andy Fastow, who now is doing ten years in the pen.

However, Serena Ng of the *Wall Street Journal* wrote that Moody's Investors Service cut credit ratings on "nearly $1 billion in bonds that were issued in 2006...because losses have risen in the pools of mortgages backing them."[47] The downgrades from investment-grade to junk-bond status came as more borrowers defaulted on their mortgages and caused losses to crest in the pools. Jay Guo, a director of asset-backed securities research at Credit Suisse Group, said in the same article, "It's unusual to see downgrades in subprime deals so soon after they were issued. This is not a normal phenomenon and is a cause of concern." The downgrades also are focusing attention on the role of credit-rating companies in the subprime downturn. Their ratings play an important part in the process of creating the bonds and in how they are valued by investors. In the *WSJ* article, Paul Ullman, chief exec of HFH Group, a New York hedge fund that is active in the mortgage market, said, "It's embarrassing for a ratings company to downgrade bonds so quickly after the bonds were issued. It reflects poorly on all parties in the underwriting process and their judgment of the credit-worthiness of the bonds."

The downgrades in recent years affected mostly bonds that were backed by speculative mortgage loans known as "second liens." These second mortgages

39

often are used by borrowers to buy homes with little or no money down. Such loans continue to experience high delinquency rates because many people stretched themselves too far financially to take them out or because these people were speculators betting on a rise in home prices. This latter category refers to investors who are engaged in "flipping." In this process, one buys a home, throws a can of paint on it, adds a few shingles, and then sells it soon after, attaining a large margin in a rising market, and especially so in a bubble market. Flipping also refers to the entrepreneur who takes on investment properties, which he or she flips or rents out, using his/her own home as collateral.

We scoff at the infomercials that advertise their packages of seminars, instruction tapes, and DVDs that will teach you how to "strike it rich in the real-estate market by buying houses with no money down!" We suggested that, if such fortunes were made so readily, then why would these RE gurus be sleeping in hotel rooms six nights per week, traveling from town to town, when they could be luxuriating on the yachts featured in their commercials? Since the publication of that article, we met a gentleman, the co-owner of a popular bar in downtown Detroit, who actually appeared in one of these infomercials. This bar owner, who prefers to remain anonymous, told us that it is not the "head cheese" who conducts all of these seminars, though he shows up for the big ones. Our source said, "I did do well in real estate, and I did appear in one of the infomercials. But, in exchange for agreeing to do the commercial, they gave me advanced instruction and showed things they don't share with the average guy who buys into the program." In addition, we believe that the instructors in this program introduced him to one of their bankers.

I grew up in the local real estate tribe and have watched many professionals and amateur dabblers make and lose money in this market. Over the last fifty years, the real-estate housing market has ebbed and flowed many times. However, the long-term average annual gain has been approximately four percent. Coincidentally, the Cost-of-Living inflation rate also has been around four percent. This means that, in the long run, one can expect housing values to keep up with inflation and not much else beyond that. However, the added value is that one enjoys a free place to live or the ability to earn rental income from a structure that holds its value over time. If you gave me $100,000 today and, at the end of fifty years, I gave you back that same amount plus interest at four percent per year but, during the interim, I let you live in my house for free, that is basically what it is all about. Maybe Glinda has waved her magic wand after all.

Chapter 9

A Mini History and Economic Lesson

"'Mankind has a rendezvous with destiny in Outer Space,' some say. We are already traveling in space. This is the galaxy, right here. The wisdom and skill of those who studied the universe first hand by direct knowledge and experience, for millennia, both inside and outside themselves, is what we might call the Old Ways. Those who envision a possible future planet on which we continue that study, and where we live by the Green and the Sun, have no choice but to bring whatever science, imagination, strength, and political finesse they have to the support of the inhibitory people—natives and peasants of the world. Entering such paths, we begin to learn a little of the Old Ways, which are outside of history, forever new."

--Gary Snyder, *The Old Ways*[18]

Myths, Legends, and Oral History

The Detroit automotive culture has many of its roots in European traditions that extend back before the Age of Serfdom. In more recent centuries, the root culture developed into a culture composed of freemen and freewomen and of people bound in servitude to the great estates as serfs (the European version of modified slavery). Let us reflect upon the gamut of family names involved in the early industry and folk history passed along by our parents and grandparents and attempt to piece together the story.

Following the breakup of the remaining tribal culture around the tenth century, many people were captured and forced into serfdom. Not all members of this earlier culture succumbed to this servitude. Remnants remained who clung to the coast of Europe where they maintained their freedom and individuality through the sea by earning a living from fishing, carrying goods upon the water, and tending to various trades along the shore. Legend has it that those of the inner court of the tribes who did not have marketable skills or trades to survive independently found themselves rounded up by roaming militia. Oral history tells us that the last of these people to go into servitude were the tribal priests, shamans, and healers who, perhaps through some natural intelligence, ability, knowledge, and charm had managed to tie themselves directly to certain kings as personal servants. While under this presumed cloak of servitude, these holy men and primitive intellectuals managed to keep alive the ancient beliefs, knowledge, and practices for nine centuries until they could fully unite once again with the free people of the coast. Serfdom finally ended for these people five or six generations ago. As they made the great migration to America, they continued to reunite here. This is the culture that found its way to the Midwest. Joining with others from additional parts of the world, it emerged as the automotive culture of Southeastern Michigan.

On 10 December 2007, we watched the CNN special report of the Nobel Peace Prize ceremonies. Following the interview with former Vice President Al Gore and the United Nations' Intergovernmental Panel on Climate Change, we began to reflect on the ramifications that the prospect of global warming has for the automotive industry in Detroit. We trust that we hardly were alone in considering not only the environmental aspects of the problem but also the economic challenge that the world's response to this growing issue brings to the automotive culture of Southeast Michigan. Given the perseverance and fortitude that marks the history of this people, we are confident that both aspects of the problem can be solved. Our conclusion is that, apart from any undue pressure from the petroleum industry to help sell their products, the Southeastern Michigan automotive industry is a culture of carriage- and wagon-makers who can equip vehicles with whatever future motive systems that the world needs. Though the internal combustion engine may continue to prove the most practical for certain bus and truck applications, there are a variety of other systems, both developed and yet to be discovered, that can be introduced for applications where alternate power systems are more necessary and desirable.

We invite you to visit the Virtual Motor City Web site at Wayne State University. When you arrive, click on Keyword Search and enter "Wilson Carriage." There you will find a photograph of thirty-five employees of the Wilson Carriage and Wagon Company from around 1900. This motley crew of somewhat scrofulous characters includes Henry Ford, Frederick J. Fisher (eldest of the seven Fisher Body brothers), and a host of other early auto-industry luminaries before they made it big. The point is that the Southeast Michigan automotive industry of today is descended from this ragtag group of carriage- and wagon-builders—the core artisans and craftsmen who defined the industry. The creation of the internal combustion engine and other forms of automotive power developed as a secondary element of this industry. If you or anyone you know can identify any of the other thirty-three Wilson employees, the Virtual Motor City project and other automotive history organizations would be most appreciative.

So, we continue to grow in our Old Ways and our New Ways, joining together science and mysticism. We move forward, improving our lives and our ways of living one small percentage point at a time. This point is typified by the development of the auto industry and the science of forensic economics. We

42

retrace the islands of time as we reach toward the stars. However, we can only move forward through eternity while the sea, the air, and the earth of our planet remain in delicate balance through the sustained rock and roll of the core and sea beneath us.

The next eleven chapters represents a chronicle—a log written while going down with the ship. In all, having a line to grasp resulted in a liberating, though painful, experience.

Chapter 10

The American Auto Industry:
The End of Ages Past

"The market was up and so was the moon. Everybody bought into the good life. Everybody was playing the game. Nobody saw what was coming."

--Commentator in "The Crash of 1929," *American Experience* series[49]

Stella, Visiting Nurse: "I was nursing a director of General Motors. Kidney ailment, they said. Nerves, I said. Then I asked myself, 'What's General Motors got to be nervous about?' Overproduction, I said—collapse! When General Motors has to go to the bathroom ten times a day, the whole country's ready to let go."

--Thelma Ritter in Alfred Hitchcock's *Rear Window*[50]

"What? Me Worry?"--Alfred E. Newman, 20th Century American Philosopher (and *Mad* Magazine Poster Boy)

For a number of years, we have listened to radio reports; watched television news features; and read interviews, commentaries, and editorials about the U.S. auto industry, specifically the Detroit auto industry. Since the end of the last major election cycle, the "If it bleeds, it leads" philosophy of journalism has led to a snowball effect in the coverage of a hemorrhaging industry, an apparent bloodletting that would put most "slasher films" to shame. In the current media blitz, everyone from sage observers like David Cole of the Center for Automotive Research to a plethora of statespersons and politicians to automotive unionist "Joe the Skilled Tradesperson" has proffered their views and advice on how to fix a problem that slowly has been coming to a boil since the 1950s—like the proverbial frog in a cooking pot.

To add our own opinions only would contribute to the metaphoric snowball as it races downhill. However, taking a Socratic position by asking rhetorical questions without providing answers beyond the muddled contents of the snowball would amount to nothing beyond intellectual arrogance. This would occur at a time when many workers have their livelihoods at stake. Therefore, we will focus our attention on many of the apparent (and a few of the obscure) issues. By doing this, we hope that our small contribution will improve a general appreciation of the problem. Furthermore, we hope that it will serve to help all of us to formulate pertinent questions and feasible answers in order to expedite the resolution of this critical problem. As context is always helpful to such ends, we will start with a thumbnail sketch of the industry as it has developed over the past 120 years before moving on to address current issues against this historical tapestry.

Early Luminaries of the Industry: A Motley Crew

As mentioned in the last chapter, one of our favorite photographs from the Virtual Motor City collection at the Wayne State University Library (dlxs.lib.wayne.edu) is a group photo of the employees of the Wilson Carriage Company. Taken on a sunny day in 1900 outside of WCC's small factory, the photo includes the scrofulous bunch of guys responsible for what would one day become the largest American industry of the twentieth century. Archivists have identified a couple of the better known personages in this photograph. In the second row, one finds a young Henry Ford in a bowler hat and ill-fitting jacket. Though he invented his first car in the early 1890s, Henry, like many other early automakers, continued to run out of funds in the effort to bring his dream to fruition. In order to "fuel" his new invention, Ford risked all of the money that he and his wife had set aside to purchase their first home. So, like his compatriots, he periodically returned to a day job at Wilson's factory. Further to the right in the same row, one sees a young Fred Fisher, who had moved to Detroit from Norfolk, Ohio. With the help of his uncle, Albert Fisher, Fred found work at Wilson's shop. Gradually, Fisher's six brothers joined him in Detroit. Through a goodly amount of perseverance and determination (not to mention $50,000 of capitalization from their Uncle Albert), the seven brothers went on to found Fisher Body Company in 1908. These are just a couple of examples from the pool of entrepreneurs who built the motorcar industry from the ground up. From 1893 to 1930, the auto industry remained highly competitive. In all, more than 1,700 small companies came and went during this era, though only a handful survived the Economic Crash of 1929.

Boom, Baby, Boom

Though the start of 1893 saw less than a dozen small companies engaged in automobile production, the number of firms grew swiftly over the next five years to more than fifty. In 1898, the auto industry generally was spread throughout Europe and a number of cities in the U.S. and Canada. However, the American industry gravitated to Southeast Michigan. In part, this aggregation occurred due to an abundance of resources, including a skilled manufacturing labor force, a supportive educational infrastructure, and numerous iron and steel works, all of which had developed in the area during the 1880s when the railroad equipment boom swept Detroit into the Industrial Age. Shortly thereafter, Detroit emerged as the loci of the industry.

A highly competitive auto industry grew rapidly over the next fifteen years until the start of World War I in 1914. Many of these were garage companies, similar in operation to garage bands in the field of rock and roll music. In an atmosphere that resembles part of the modern Detroit rock 'n' roll scene, two-thirds of small car companies did not continue production beyond three years. Furthermore, only ten percent remained active for more than five years, while only five percent survived for more than twelve years.

During this decade and a half of intense growth, competition rose rapidly, while the price of automobiles fell sharply. As with most new products, the auto started as a high-priced luxury good, affordable only to the most affluent. However, as competition increased and prices fell, small-volume producers who lacked sufficient economies of scale found themselves squeezed between high manufacturing and distribution costs per vehicle and rapidly falling market price. Similar to production in the PC computer industry a decade ago, many manufacturers merely assembled parts, designed and produced by other companies, and then affixed their own nameplates to the front of the radiators. These car companies experienced the highest production costs. In a race toward survival, numerous small automakers merged with one another while others sold their works outright to more stable producers. However, many firms simply closed their doors and sold off their assets to new entrants who were willing to try their hand at making horseless carriages.

"I Have Seen the Future, and Its Name is Electric!"
During this era of entrepreneurship and experimentation, companies with exotic names like Bugmobile and Vixen came and went from the scene. Among the many cars created, vehicles powered by electricity, steam, and gasoline were produced. Scrolling through a list of extinct companies offers proof that there is nothing really new under the sun. One even finds examples of dual-powered cars—hybrids of gas and electric power.

In his book *Internal Combustion: How Corporations and Government Addicted the World to Oil and Derailed the Alternatives*,[51] Edwin Black states that Henry Ford envisioned the future of the automobile as electric. In 1914, Ford joined together with his friend Thomas Edison to form an electric car company. However, even though Ford and Edison may have seen the future as electric, others apparently did not. After a mysterious fire destroyed his Menlo Park laboratory, Edison, who was developing new efficient electric cells, became despondent and dropped out of the electric car business. Subsequently, Ford turned his attention to mass producing his black gas-powered flivver—the Model T. An eighty-year sequence of historic events would continue to suppress the development of alternate sources for transportation fuel.

The number of small-firm automakers that actively produced in any given year mushroomed from fifty in 1898 to more than 340 by 1914. However, that count dropped in half by the end of the First World War. Following a brief four-year post-war resurgence, the number of independent car makers declined steadily throughout the 1920s. Through acquisition, merger, and failure, the industry grew more and more concentrated. The falling unit costs associated with mass production drove this concentration. When Wall Street finally laid an egg in October, 1929, this left less than seventy companies in existence. Though a few new small companies appeared sporadically during the succeeding decades, the Detroit firms that have managed to survive to this day emerged from the Great Depression and World War II as part of a tight oligopoly market that finally became the "Big Three."

"Big Auto" Goes to War

The Second World War proved most beneficial to the recovering automotive industry. The war economy pushed the remaining automotive producers toward an even tighter oligopolistic market structure as contracts for military hardware came from the U.S. government. Arms production led to a massive rise in employment from which the Detroit firms realized a three-fold increase in size during the first half of the 1940s. Following the wartime destruction of much of the productive capacity of both Europe and Japan, the Detroit Oligopoly entered the 1950s with 90% of the world's automobile market. The Detroit firms maintained a high level of employment that many spectators close to the industry referred to as the absorption of the surplus labor force—that segment of workers who were displaced during the 1930s and were absorbed by the military during the war. The employment of this segment afforded political currency to the auto oligopoly as they faced off over charges of excessive market concentration. In the mid-1950s, the U.S. Justice Department invoked a threat to break General Motors, and possibly Ford, into a number of smaller companies. However, the industry pointed out that such an action would lead to the further displacement of the surplus labor force. Apparently, a deal was cut. The outcome of this episode was that the Detroit Oligoply remained intact as it entered the 1960s.

To paraphrase singer/songwriter Bob Dylan, "The times they were a-changin'." Gradually, over the next few decades, European producers bolstered their international market share while Japan transformed its domestic production from bicycles to motor bikes and then to automobiles. During the 1960s, high gasoline taxes led to high prices at the pump in Europe and other parts of the world. This market condition was accompanied by relatively low disposable incomes among consumers. This led to automobile customers in Europe and along the Pacific Rim voicing their preferences for smaller, more fuel-efficient vehicles. However, Americans continued to demand larger, expensive automobiles.

Gasoline constitutes the primary complementary good to automobiles. Whenever prices at the pump increase, the demand for large, less fuel-efficient autos significantly decreases. Conversely, the demand for more fuel-efficient ones increases. Since the early days of the industry, this very simple economic model has empowered the oil oligopoly both economically and politically, giving it power over decisions by and for the automotive industry.

In the early 1970s, U.S. consumers responded to the price surges brought about by the O.P.E.C. Oil Crisis. Facing shortages that led to escalating fuel prices, American consumers began to demand more fuel-efficient cars. Having developed such products for their own domestic markets, foreign automakers found themselves in the cat-bird seat while U.S. producers rushed to catch up with the rapidly changing market. Gradually, Detroit's "Big Three" regained competitive strength and adapted to the newly expanding global marketplace by developing smaller vehicles. Ford built off of its Anglia production base in England while GM moved forward from its Opel base in Germany—a toe-hold that the company has retained since before World War II.

With world politics of the oil business being what they are, pump prices grew more affordable relative to income over the next two decades. Credit markets expanded to meet the demands of a more educated and affluent Baby Boomer generation. The frugality and fuel-consciousness of the 1970s began to give way to the excesses of an age of SUVs and consumerism. This was supported by rising home values, the further expansion of consumer credit, and a growing trend of deregulation. In his book *The New Paradigm for Financial Markets: The Credit Crisis of 2008 and What It Means*,[52] George Soros explains that this multiplicity of events spawned a Super Bubble in the early 1980s that has lasted twenty-five years. However, Soros asserts that this bubble is rapidly approaching the bursting point. Since the 1980s, this mega-bubble has carried a series of smaller bubbles on its back. To be graphic, we have witnessed a succession of conglomeration, high-tech, and mortgage bubbles, all of which have burst like a series of zits atop a festering boil.

During the past few decades, China, India, and other formerly back-seat nations have moved to riding shotgun in the car that is the global economy. Even though the majority of their populations remain underclass, the western-educated elite enjoy first-world affluence. The sheer size of the total population of these countries means that the small percentage riding on the hoods of their socio-economic vehicles constitutes a significant consumer force in the global market. This large emerging group continues to drive up the demand for automobiles and the gasoline that runs them.

All of these events of the past century have contributed to the dire straits in which the U.S. auto industry now finds itself. Let us stand back and appreciate the situation for a moment.

Merger, Merger, Merger—Poking a Wasps' Nest with a Stick

Talk of mergers illumined the night skies last fall. For the first time in the past six decades, the "Big Three" market share stopped bumping against the wall of our Antitrust Laws. Given the disjuncture of Chrysler from Daimler, coupled with the gradual gain in U.S. market share by Toyota and other foreign-based firms, the combined remaining market share of the Detroit Oligopoly has dropped to almost half of its 1950s high-water mark. Now that their combined share has dropped below the Antitrust Law radar, mergers and buyouts of company fragments appear as realistic prospects.

However, just because an event *can* occur legally does not necessarily mean that it *should* occur. Ford has held itself back recently from merger negotiations with the hope of approaching such a possibility from a position of strength. On the other hand, Chrysler has found itself in a predicament stemming from their merger with, and subsequent buyout from, Daimler. The private investment firm of Cerberus has entered the arena by acquiring an 80% hold on Chrysler while at the same time exerting great leverage upon short-of-cash General Motors through a 51% control of the GMAC financial group.

The proposed merger gives the appearance of a Gordon Gekko-style takeover.[53] This pen-rattling points to the gleaning away of the Jeep line while shutting down the remainder of production. At first blanch, this proposed purchase seems to be a very costly way to obtain this one desirable property. In an era of excess capacity throughout the industry, an acquisition of Chrysler's assets would necessitate taking on the burden of a copious amount of real estate. It is important to note that such property likely will hold little, if any, value. Furthermore, it would seem that the last thing that GM, not to mention Detroit, needs are large tracts of unused property that lingers and deteriorates like the decaying Packard Plant. These ruins stand only as a testimonial to the spiders, rats, and pigeons on Detroit's near-East side—not good for public relations and *especially* not good for the pocketbook.

More fundamentally, we need to consider the long-run impacts of any decisions. Our vision needs to extend well beyond the quarterly time frame upon which company managers must focus in order to fulfill their fiduciary responsibilities. Furthermore, the long-run that we must consider extends way beyond a five- or ten-year period. The necessary vision must consider the multi-century stability, growth, and development of a complex or stakeholders who settled on this land a century-and-half ago. We are only in the first quarter of an 800- to 1200-year epic game. This extensive time frame reflects the process of migration, cultural re-establishment, growth, decline, and successive migration. Though long accepted and understood in other parts of the world, this time frame continues to be viewed quixotically in this country. However, we need to learn to think collectively in these terms.

At the core of each of the three metropolitan Detroit auto firms stands what sociologists refer to as a kindred network. Composed of many small and large extended families, these networks have evolved quietly over the past few generations. Remaining at a low profile, each one involves a network of families that have been, and continue to be, involved as labor, management, and stockholders of significant blocks of preferred and common stock. In the case of General Motors, the combination of a few large blocks of stock held by its kindred network represents the majority of interests. Perhaps because of the family name, the kindred group and majority holdings at Ford are more obvious. However, in respect to Chrysler, the Daimler merger and subsequent sell-off has obscured the transparency of the holdings and may have disrupted the impact that its core kindred network long maintained.

The reluctance of these core kindred groups to divest themselves of their collective holdings has posed a juggernaut to Kirk Kerkorian and similar interlopers. Eventually, these people turned away when they experienced this substantial barrier to entry during their efforts to acquire control of the auto companies. However, given the rather rocky and (as some have termed it) subservient stature that Chrysler held as hausfrau to Daimler, perhaps it would prove advisable to consult with the Chrysler kindred network along with those of General Motors and Ford before any major decisions are finalized. After all, they do constitute the three major lines of the same "tribe." A "shotgun wedding," as the press has called it, may stir up more problems for all parties concerned in both the short- and long-runs. In fact, the cost may exceed what the deal is worth.

The Case for National Defense

For more than a century, the manufacture of automotive products in Southeast Michigan has encouraged the concentration of physical and intellectual capital toward the purpose of developing exceptional manufacturing capabilities. This movement has continued consistently since the era of railroad equipment manufacturing in the decades following the War Between the States. This intense focus on manufacturing has led to the development of a knowledge- and skills-based culture that has spilled beyond the workplace and schools and into the backyards and basements of family homes. Children have been raised in this culture, learning about tools from parents, grandparents, and older siblings. They develop labor skills by tinkering with mini-bikes, go-carts, and other mechanical wonders built from spare parts and scrap in the family garage. In addition, they participate in events such as the Soap Box Derby, which was sponsored for many years by the *Detroit News*. All of these cultural "growth exercises" have served to root multiple generations in the fundamentals of manufacturing. This constitutes a social wealth that cannot be emulated elsewhere without significant effort and passage of time.

The "what" that we produce in Southeast Michigan is secondary to the inherent process of production. This process that emanates from the core of our culture stems from the synergetic interaction of family, work, education, and involvement in various value-oriented and spiritual-development groups.

It is the preservation of continued cultural growth rather than the production of any specific product that constitutes the real wealth of our region, our country, and our world. However, the practical matter necessary for continued growth and development requires that our labor force and educational institutions continue to have a product to produce. Therefore, on the occasions on which we are called upon to produce for the cause of national defense, we are prepared. Why? We have a solid manufacturing culture. Furthermore, we hope that a situation never will arise that would force the U.S. to rely upon the "kindness of strangers,"[54] one in which we must turn to other nations to supply tools for our own protection, as our European allies were forced to do during the Second World War.

In the next chapter, we will continue our discussion of this topic. We will address such issues as employee compensation and benefits for the rank-and-file hourly workers as well as the highest level of management/intrapreneurs. Within the context developed above, we will consider the prospects of government participation with the industry in the form of short-term bail-outs as well as longer-term partnering. Also, we will consider the impact of the transformation to alternate fuel sources along with potential obstacles that either could save or destroy the industry. Finally, we will discuss the possibility and feasibility of separating overseas operations from domestic production along with other "What-if?" scenarios that could unleash a flurry of lawsuits in the arenas of intellectual property, labor, contract, antitrust, stockholder rights, and other law.

Chapter 11

The American Auto Industry:
The Prelude to the Future

"It's a recession when your neighbor loses his job; it's a depression when you lose yours."
--Harry S. Truman, 33rd President of the United States

In chapter ten, we focused on the history of how the Detroit automotive industry developed over a century ago and how it came to its current predicament. That was easy. The target stood still. In this chapter, we will address the matter of what can be done, what should be done, and the ramifications of any such actions. This target is moving as we write.

"It Is Not the Return *on* My Investment I am Concerned about; It Is the Return *of* My Investment." – Will Rogers, 20th Century American Humorist

It has become obvious to most Americans that something must be done to solve the current crisis that besets the auto industry, a crisis that is due to the vast spillover effect on the rest of our economy. However, the real question remains as to whether or not it is more desirable and feasible for the industry itself, and those with vested interests, to solve the auto industry's problems without outside assistance. Alternately, should the Federal and other levels of government step in and solve these problems with immediate finality? Alternately, should they continue to develop some mutually comprehensive approach that engages interests of both the private and public sectors?

The country and Congress remains split as to whether private sector interests can, or would, find a solution on their own that would prove satisfactory to all stakeholders. Many people seem to feel that it is likely that labor and outside stockholders would get screwed in the deal. Furthermore, others doubt whether or not the government could--or should--achieve the same ends by itself. Many people doubt that agencies of the Federal government have the coordination and insight to step in and manage a situation so shrouded in secretive complexity while continuing to fulfill its fiduciary responsibility to the American taxpayer.

Lacking viable alternatives, this may leave the bi-lateral effort in which we are currently embroiled as the only feasible approach for coming to a timely copasetic solution. However, given the current state of national and global economic conditions, such an approach must not only be swift but accurate and transparent. These characteristics must be part of the solution if we wish for all parties to walk away from the table with mutual, optimal satisfaction.

"The Opera Isn't Over Until Brunhilde Sings" (Attributed to the Last Scene of Richard Wagner's Opera, *Die Walkure*)

What lingers on the table like unplucked Christmas geese are four distinct possible approaches: 1) Billions of dollars of debt or equity investment from the private and/or public sector to sustain the industry until the market for automotive products improves and the companies at risk can restructure satisfactorily to meet whatever that future market may bring. 2) Let the auto companies enter into either a Congressional Oversight Agreement (satisfactory) or a Chapter Eleven Bankruptcy proceedings (less desirable) that would force the companies to renegotiate their contracts and to realign other structural elements under the supervision of Congress or Federal Court. 3) Allow the companies to enter into Chapter Seven Bankruptcy proceedings, the least desirable approach; this effectively would shut them down and force a liquidation of remaining assets of spurious value. 4) Continue attempts to develop a plan that combines the first and second approaches; this would include an immediate influx of capital under governmental oversight and management.

A Bridge Is More Than a Transition between a Verse and a Chorus

Any of us who have committed to purchasing a new home while still selling our present home likely have encountered the concept of a bridge loan. The purpose of such a loan is to allow a homeowner to make mortgage payments simultaneously on both properties without undue stress until the current property finally sells. Typically, lenders justify such a financial arrangement as long as the current property maintains its value until sold. However, if the current property decreases significantly in value, the lender loses the incentive to make or to continue the bridge loan in the face of evaporating collateral. In relation to the current crisis facing auto companies, the point is this: what may start out as a bridge loan quickly could turn into a failed bail-out if other macroeconomic market conditions remain unstable. The direct impact of companies burning through cash secured through additional debt would result in the destruction of any remaining stockholder equity as the companies slide into insolvency.

54

"Betelgeuse, Betelgeuse, Betelgeuse!"[55]

This matter turns to the demand side, one of expediently increasing revenues. Therefore, as addressed in the recent Congressional hearings, the credit markets must be freed up. We repeat with great feeling: The credit markets must be freed up! The credit markets must be freed up! The two largest expenditures made by American families are for housing and automobiles. Both industries directly employ and indirectly effect the employment of a major segment of our labor force. Consumer spending by all strata of workers in these two industries drives the U.S. economy. Though some individuals can afford to pay cash for a new home or car, most people must rely upon the availability of consumer credit to make these large purchases. Furthermore, the multitude of small businesses in the country, including real estate and mortgage brokerages and auto dealerships, rely upon business lines of credit to smooth their cash flow and meet their week-to-week obligations. Congress rapidly approved the $750 billion package for the financial industry in a non-transparent and loosely regulated way because Americans thought that it would free up consumer credit. Are we wrong to assume that American taxpayers believed that this bail-out package would benefit them directly? If the private financial sector, which has been enabled by taxpayers, remains unable or unwilling to free up this credit, then the U.S. government needs to pull this funding back immediately. The government needs to make this funding available directly to our citizenry through programs modeled after those of the mid-twentieth century, such as the FHA and GI Bill.

The automotive industry always has responded to the whims of the market. When gasoline was consistently less expensive, a new generation of customers demanded what we might call "fancy family trucks" (SUVs). The good news is that they are well built and should last for many years as family vehicles. The bad news is that they are well built and should last for many years, such that future demand for replacement units will continue to fall. A Hummer is a great vehicle for a contractor who puts it in heavy use, such as visiting off-road construction sites. However, such vehicles pose a bit of overkill for an urban/suburban resident who uses one to go grocery shopping or to run errands. Why are we surprised if demand declines?

Similar to the market that followed the OPEC crisis of the early 1970s, customers have once again begun to applaud smaller fuel-efficient cars. Granted, the world is going through a paradigm shift in terms of the kinds of technologies that we need. The auto industry has responded by developing new lines of vehicles. However, can the industry transcend the chasm of time that exists until the new technologies sustain a steady profit stream? The electrics will not hit the market until 2010 or later. Barring unforeseen factors, these new lines may not emerge as profitable for three to five years after their introduction. Therefore, until a point in time between 2013 or 2015, these new products need cross-collateralization through the sale of larger vehicles that use traditional technologies. However, market demand for these products has been declining. This leaves the companies with excess productive capacity. Is there a problem, Houston?

Are we missing something?

It Ain't Over 'til the Fat Lady Sings" (Attributed to Victorian-Era Engineers Pulling into Paddington Station, London)

Detroit's manufacturing history predates the automotive industry. During the quarter-century following the American Civil War, Detroit flourished as the railroad-manufacturing capital of the world. Companies in the area produced the greatest annual footage of steel rail anywhere. In addition, local firms produced a variety of rolling stock, including locomotives and freight and passenger cars. Building the country's transportation infrastructure during the Great Westward Expansion created a substantial boom period. However, this boom was not sustainable due to market saturation for products that had a slow obsolescence. Subsequently, Detroit survived as the stove capital of the world for the decade between the Railroad and Automotive Ages.

The point is that Detroit exists as a heavy-metal manufacturing city, not just a car-assembly town. Furthermore, Detroit manufacturers have proven their ability to adapt rapidly to changing circumstances. The best example followed the bombing of Pearl Harbor. Congress proved itself capable of bipartisan cooperation for national interests. Within a month, it passed legislation that led to the conversion of auto factories to tank and airplane production almost overnight.

Though we currently do not face acts of aggression of a comparable intensity, America does face the reality of a decaying infrastructure in areas that include transportation and national defense. If we can expect the Detroit manufacturing community to have excess productive capacity for the next decade, why not put it to good use? Whenever any business finds itself with an excess of labor time, equipment, and buildings, the opportunity exists to cut some great deals, not only for the public but for manufacturers and their tiers of suppliers. The Detroit manufacturing base does not need or want a handout. However, it does need a hand. Doesn't the opportunity present itself for the Federal, state, and local governments to take advantage of deals that would prove advantageous to the entire nation as well as to Detroit. Put out the banners! This is the time for bargains.

However, the possibility of temporary conversion to infrastructure manufacturing does not preclude the need to restructure the automotive industry into a form that can remain viable in the face of a changing global marketplace and perilous natural conditions on our planet. Therefore, the concept of how to accomplish this restructure remains on par with the actual restructuring itself. Granted, contracting for infrastructure work would provide the economic rationale for any series of mergers, acquisitions, divestitures, or other reconfigurations. However, we should not consider such a course an opportunity to belay problems that have developed over the past half-century. Instead, we would need to approach this course as an opportunity to buy some time in order to achieve lasting and sustainable results.

"Forget the Fat Lady. You're Obsessed with the Fat Lady."[56]

The erosion that has undermined the auto industry affects 10% of our national employment. It runs from the top of the industrial hierarchy down through its core to the very bottom. In this respect, compensation and benefits comprise much of the shifting sand. We doubt that any normal person savors the idea of scaling back. However, we must consider the essence of pay. The amount that anyone can expect in terms of compensation and benefits must reflect the real value of his or her product in the final market. The amount of income that anyone can expect to earn must be derived from a rational expectation of the realized revenue that the final product will bring from the market. This should be coupled with the degree of productivity exhibited by any and all in the creation of that product.

Separating current compensation from fringe benefits and deferred compensation largely reflects an easement of cash flow for the firm and an opportunity for tax savings to the employee. Pensions constitute a deferred payment that benefits both employer and employee. The amount of pension is money that is owed to the employee—no ifs, ands, or buts. To explain it simply, let us say that I offer you $30.00 to perform some work for me. If I give you the entire $30.00 today, you will have to pay the full tax on it today. However, if I only give you $20.00 today, your present tax bill will be lower and you will receive the other $10.00 at a later date when your tax rate is lower—a win-win arrangement, right?

Health insurance bears similarities as well as differences in respect to pension benefits. Purchasing health insurance costs less per employee when purchased in a group. Historically, when employers have paid for the insurance to the benefit of their employee, the amount paid has not counted as taxable income to the employee. However, to fully understand health insurance as a job benefit in America, we must look at its strange history. During World War II, health care and other benefits quickly became popular among employers as a means to circumvent wage freezes imposed by the Federal government as it attempted to control wartime inflation. During this time of labor shortages, Federal law prohibited employers from offering wage premiums in order to lure workers away from other firms. However, no prohibition existed that forbade offering a non-taxable fringe benefit as the carrot. So, by the end of the war, health insurance had become a standard benefit paid by most large employers.

However, the situation has changed. In countries other than the U.S., national health care developed as public programs for historical reasons, such as political climate, labor parties ascending to power in governments, and a basic need for public health after World War II. American firms now find themselves competing in a global economy against foreign national companies with lower cost structures. A significant part of that cost differential lies in the fact that employees from other countries are covered by health-care plans provided by their own governments. Our own domestic workforce does not enjoy the same benefit from our government. This results in higher costs for American companies. Our own system for providing health-insurance coverage that once proved to have an enormous competitive benefit has taken a 180-degree shift. Now, our system has impaired our ability to compete in the global economy. The U.S. government can best serve all of our globally competitive industries by solving the lingering problems inherent in our health-care infrastructure decisively. Indeed, if part of the role of our government remains to serve as the leveler of the proverbial playing field for the private sector, then shifting the burden of health care for employees and retirees would prove a grand move toward this goal of leveling our playing field.

"You Want a Friend in Washington? Get a Dog." – Harry S. Truman

Of course, all of this governmental assistance will prove nil unless the auto industry fixes itself from the top down and the bottom up. The problems of the auto industry are reflective of those of Corporate America in general. A series of systemic problems has resulted from a quarter century of deregulation. This has left any healthy power in Corporate America whacked out of balance. In effect, the hired help has taken over and looted the store! As glorious as CEOs with MBAs appear to the public, most remain employees in corporate structures previously developed by earlier entrepreneurs. These managers are not entrepreneurs who often risk everything to create a new business. They are hired help who have the fiduciary responsibility to keep the company in balance as a profitable growing concern. In the best cases, CEOs, CFOs, COOs and other officers may step forward as intrapreneurs that further develop existing businesses. In such cases, they are entitled to share in the spoils that they help to create—if, and only if, they realize a gain for the company! Granted, hired managers often perform difficult jobs. However, the just desserts that they receive for their efforts must return to being just desserts in fairness and balance to all of the other employees as well as to all other stockholders.

That being said, demands made by Congress for CEOs like Rick Wagoner of General Motors to "move on" will not solve the problems inherent to GM or any similarly situated corporation. GM invested many years into Wagoner's knowledge, experience, and skill base. However, problems are caused when a manager wears too many hats. Not uncommon to Corporate America, Mr. Wagoner served as both the CEO and the Chairman of the Board of Directors of General Motors. If not by the word of the law, then at least in the spirit, such a double role violates the basic rule of separation of function. Before finally stepping down, Wagoner told the Congressional Committee that, as CEO, he serves at the pleasure of the Board. However, as the Chairman of the Board, he and other high-level managers have shaped the Board into a rubber-stamp organization that applauds their agenda but fails to represent the broad base of vested stakeholders. Only by breaking this logjam at GM and other firms throughout Corporate America can any meaningful, sustainable change begin to develop. As Forrest Gump would say in the movie of the same name, "That's all I have to say about that."[57]

So how does all of this affect attorneys and economists? There will be a great demand for work in fields such as Contract Law, Labor Law, Intellectual Property, and Shareholder Rights. However, attorneys and their academic cohorts may find themselves going to work on horseback.

Chapter 12

In the Decline of the Industrial Age

"Winter time is a hard time for a change / It's the time to collect all our thoughts once again. All the means of production / All the ways of destruction / All society's wealth inside ourselves."
--John Sase, "Winter Song," *Aessence*[58]

Buddy, Can You Spare a Dime?

When Congress came to the aid of General Motors and Chrysler in December 2008, their funneling of taxpayer funds into the auto companies bought some time—at least until the cold weather broke in March 2009. In order to save jobs in Southeastern Michigan as well as to prevent the collapse of two of the three domestic automakers, Congress gave these companies ninety days to come up with a workable plan for their own salvation.

Though the auto industry has been barreling down the highway known as Desolation Row (to paraphrase Bob Dylan) for the past twenty-five years, two major short-term forces have brought the companies to a grinding halt. The consumer price of gasoline at the pump in 2008 and the lack of credit to consumers, suppliers, dealers, and the companies themselves would have made it virtually impossible to weather this winter storm without the intervention of Congress.

The rapid drop in pump prices over the past few months suggest that the high prices of last summer resulted more from a speculative bubble in the crude-oil market than from a surge in consumer demand for gasoline. Nevertheless, the bubble took its toll on automakers, especially those supporting less fuel-efficient product lines.

However, the credit market is another story. Here, money remains tight for all parties concerned. Word has come through that the Senate passed the $838 billion Economic Stimulus plan by a margin of sixty-one to thirty-seven votes. Recent polls have indicated that only slightly more than half of the American public supports the Congressional plans. A major question on the minds of many people is, "How are we going to finance the $838 billion (Senate) or $820 billion (House) packages that have emerged as low-fat alternatives to the high calorie plans of the past?" Then, we need to throw Health Care financing into the mixer as well.

To understand these plans, we need to weigh them as investments rather than expenses. The old business adage of "It takes money to make money" probably holds true for lifting ourselves out of this intense economic milieu. Therefore, we should regard and manage the stimulus as an investment in America's future economy rather than another fill-the-gap spending program. However, the question remains as to how to finance this plan. Should we create more money through the Federal Reserve System and financial community and risk the inflationary effects that would come with monetizing the proposals? Alternately, should the U.S. Treasury issue additional securities and engage in debt financing that will require extensive borrowing from our own citizens as well as from investors in other countries? The funds for this government investment must come from someplace, but from where? Furthermore, many of us need to know the payback period and the expected rate of return on this investment. Don't get us wrong. We generally agree with President Obama on the necessity and immediacy of this action. Let us just make sure that this program is better managed than the original Troubled Assets Relief Program that the previous administration rushed through over a weekend.

In the meantime, consumer confidence has continued to stall through 2009 while unemployment has reach long-term highs in many states. Even foreign transplants like Nissan and Toyota are being hit hard throughout the global marketplace as automotive sales swirl in the proverbial toilet bowl. Propped up by taxpayer money, Chrysler sought and won an alliance with Fiat, a non-domestic (Italian) company, to gain access to small-car technology. However, this runs against the grain of Congressional oversight by decreasing transparency. As with Daimler before, this deal involves a foreign national—a corporation that is not required to file a 10-Q, 10-K, or any other periodic financial disclosures to the U.S. public through the Securities Exchange Commission. Already, the Chrysler situation has lacked transparency as Cerberus, a private equity firm, held controlling interest in the company.

However, in all fairness, we must note that Congress required Chrysler to liquidate its foreign product lines as a condition of the governmental bailout of 1980. In contrast, GM and Ford have continued to hold a number of foreign subsidiary lines such as Opel and Anglia for most of the past century. To remain competitive—to continue to exist!—Chrysler must quickly acquire and introduce small-vehicle technologies (beyond the Smart Car) to counter its failing large vehicle markets.

Chrysler LLC, under the ownership of Cerberus Capital Management, currently remains semi-transparent while Ford Motor Company, in contrast, has only one foot stuck in the quagmire. Therefore, we turn our attention to General Motors Corporation as our primary subject of analysis.

"I Could Be President of General Motors, Baby, Hey, or Just a Tiny Little Grain of Sand"
--Al Kooper, "I Love You More Than You'll Ever Know," Blood Sweat and Tears, *Child is Father to the Man*[59]

What is to become of General Motors? As a child in the mid-1950s, I (Dr. Sase) listened to my elders as they proffered what they foresaw down the road, fifty years into the future. Were they clairvoyant? Perhaps. However, it is more likely their foresight simply may have been derived from the sage advice of their own elders as history repeats itself. This accumulated tribal knowledge was coupled with my elders' own life experience of growing up during the era when the auto industry emerged in the first quarter of the twentieth century and then slid through the Depression of the 1930s. So, as I write of these matters, I largely base my perspective upon the fragments of wisdom that I recall from conversations overheard a half-century ago.

We are certain that the collective ego of GM can survive the "stigma" of being the *second*-largest automaker. However, in these harsh times, GM certainly finds it more important simply to remain an automaker in some form.

While not intending to play the preschool thespian role of "Johnny Rain Cloud," we do need to remove the smoke and mirrors that surround General Motors. Throughout early 2009, many stakeholders, a term that now includes all American taxpayers, watched patiently to see if GM and the other domestic automakers would be solvent.

Sorry to break the news to you, folks, but GM had been insolvent since at least early 2008. The share price of its common stock had been artificially sustained by paying a twenty-five cent dividend per share. (This dividend decreased from fifty cents in February 2006.) However, in the recent past, this dividend has been drawn from equity. More recently, it has come from debt financing (robbing Peter to pay Paul?) as the company has not seen any consolidated earnings for a number of quarters. Finally GM cancelled their dividend in 2008.

The reported Price-to-Earnings ratio stands at zero! Actually, we consider this statement misleading, as P/E ratios are not usually reported as negative values. Mathematically, dividing the current market price (at 3:34 PM on 10 February 2009) of $2.77 by earnings of zero results in an undefined value. In effect, the common stock is behaving more like a bond if it were to continue to pay a constant dollar return to investors. At a price of $2.77 per share, this now passé return on investment would equal a solid 9.0%. As long as GM continued to pay this "dividend," the common stock shares mystically continued to hold a positive value for investors. However, if GM follows the Congressional mandate to continue its "no dividend policy" as part of the rescue plan, then the floor would (and did) cease to exist to stop the share price from plummeting toward zero. (Note: Even after the stock was delisted from the stock exchange, the bid-price for worthless shares remained above zero due to some animal spirit speculation.)

How long did it take for share price to collapse completely? From a relative high of $38.22 per share on 30 October 2007, the market price generally has declined asymptotically (decreasing at a decreasing rate toward zero). Put in simple terms, GM share price declined by more than 92% in fifteen months. Currently, the company is being kept alive only through artificial respiration.

Our independent observations and analyses contributed a little new information to an ongoing discussion. However, back on 8 November 2008, Swedish economist Stefan Karlsson noted in his blog that "GM now has negative equity--and we're not talking about small sums. ...[O]n June 30 [2008], General Motors had assets to the value of $136 billion and liabilities of $193 billion, implying a negative equity of $57 billion! And with the loss they reported for the third quarter, equity is presumably even more negative now. And given how dire the outlook is for car sales, can anything but increased losses be expected?" Karlsson concludes by stating, "General Motors should have been declared bankrupt for some time now."[60] The bailout (bridge loan) that Congress bestowed would have needed to be repaid if the company had not pieced together a workable solution by late March 2009. As a result, the question for taxpayers may become one of how to get blood from a stone? (Note: Anne Boleyn's headsman suggests that boiling often works if the blood has not thoroughly dried.)

So is General Motors nothing more than a floating corpse? Perhaps. However, the corporation continues to remain an extremely large, capital-intensive entity. If its plant, equipment, and intellectual property are not product-specific assets in themselves, they do exist, at least, as industry-specific assets. What this means in the real world is that GM's major assets (real and intellectual properties) only have value as long as someone continues to work with them. Furthermore, given that many other automakers around the world are bereft with surplus capacity and hold comparable or superior intellectual property, not much of a market may exist for any industry-specific plant, equipment, and intellectual property that could be gleaned from the corpse. Therefore, a resurrection from the ashes may prove the only rational solution. For economic shamans, the question remains: how do we raise the animal spirits?

"We Must Find New Solutions / to Ways We Defend / Earth Takes Retribution / in These Days of End."
--John Sase, "Decline of the Industrial Age," *Aessence*[61]

If we observe how other industries have restructured to survive, we may find many useful, though "not-created-here," solutions. As with any durable goods business, a few major challenges present themselves to the auto industry. These include design and engineering, adequate capitalization, and, perhaps foremost, distribution. Let us start with distribution.

Product distribution remains fundamental to the success of the auto industry. In the early days of the industry, many short-lived, small competitive companies vanished into the pages of automotive history because they simply lacked adequate distribution to get their product known and into the hands of prospective customers. Granted, low production volume and the accompanying lack of economies of scale contributed to their woes. However, along with these contributing factors, a lack of adequate channels of distribution meant that two-thirds of the more than 300 makes of automobiles produced in 1910 would not survive in the market for more than a few years. Of the more fortunate ones, less than six percent would endure for more than a decade.

With relatively low differentiation among many makes and models of their product, General Motors actually exists as a "brand portal." Perhaps, this attribute remains its greatest value. Just as specific, unique images come to mind when one hears the brand portal names of Disney or Motown, the identity associated with the name General Motors produces its own set of unique images. Over the past century, GM has built its distribution chain by developing and maintaining relationships with consumers through the vast network of dealers who are members of their own brand portal, the North American Auto Dealers Association (NADA).

In this new century, companies like Disney and Motown in the film and music industries generally have abandoned the business model of vertical integration for creating the products flowing through their brand portals. Perhaps establishing General Motors (and the other auto giants) as separate distribution companies that contract and finance the development of product from a series of competitive independent vehicle producers would present a viable solution to the current predicament.

Next, let us turn to design and engineering. In addition to underlying research and development, design and engineering entails matters of intellectual property (IP). These matters largely involve the sharing of, and the legal protection of, these properties. To address the needs of America as well as the needs of the rest of the planet, research and development must be intensified and expanded to find new, sustainable technologies for the future.

No one company alone can meet this challenge adequately. Therefore, we suggest an alliance between various levels of government, private and public universities, and a private sector research and development company split off of the present corporation. Through the half-utilized GM Tech Center campus and its satellites, a newly created entity could feed the basic developments in new technologies protected as intellectual property into the realm of design and engineering. In turn, under further IP protection, the engineering and design work could be licensed to the set of independent production companies. Such a plan may address the challenges of the next few critical decades.

On the financial side of this picture, we have the remains of the General Motors Acceptance Corporation (GMAC). As with similar structures at the other auto companies, GMAC was originally formed in 1919 "to provide GM dealers with the financing they needed to maintain their vehicle inventories as well as give dealers' retail customers the ability to purchase new vehicles easily and conveniently."[62] Many may argue that GMAC lost its focus when it first entered the mortgage business in 1985. Others would argue that GMAC further aggravated the situation in the 1990s when it purchased the Bank of New York's asset-based lending and factoring business unit to create its new Commercial Finance Group.

In 2006, Cerberus purchased a controlling fifty-one percent of GMAC from GM. The sudden impact of the change of hands exerted a higher toll on its focus. Furthermore, in 2008, Cerberus Capital Management LP expressed its interest in acquiring full ownership of GMAC Financial Services in order to merge it with Chrysler Financial, which it acquired in its deal with Daimler AG. According to Maryann Keller, a longtime auto industry analyst and head of Maryann Keller & Associates, "If this were to take place, the winner would be Cerberus, which would benefit by combining the financial operations."[63]

However, a window of opportunity to refocus began to open in October 2008. Discussions between GM and Cerberus appear to confirm recent speculation that Cerberus desires to withdraw from the deteriorating U.S. auto industry. In all, GMAC presents a major challenge to this donnybrook if this newly chartered bank (now eligible to receive Federal financial bailout money) is ever to return to its primary mission. Whether or not the credit/financial entity remains in the form of GMAC or emerges as some other newly created or acquired entity, the automaker needs a company that can extend credit to dealers, retail customers, and the proposed group of independent producers. However, by summer of 2009 the three-headed hound that guards the gates of Hades was foraging around to save what it could of its holdings in Chrysler Financial.

Now we turn to the fourth leg of our stool—the proposed group of independent production companies. Given that the corporate equity has fallen into the hole and the stock is virtually worthless (or at least below water as so many homeowners equity may be), a transfer of major blocks of holdings appears almost as an academic exercise. The heart of the industry remains the production of vehicles. Though auto production is less glamorous but more capital-intensive than most other businesses, the automotive industry cannot continue to exist without successful vehicle manufacturing. Breaking off the sum of GM production into a single company or a series of competing companies means transferring the responsibility for its survival to a consortium of owner-operators. In other words, give the business to a group, or back to a group, of extended families that can make a go of it and ensure its survival.

This concludes our proposal. By breaking one entity into four separate pieces, we have represented only one of many possible ideas to turn around this vital industry. Hopefully, those who would critique this proposal at least will find it a catalyst for generating a series of feasible alternatives.

When the economy falls into turmoil, questions arise regarding the setting of precedents for issues that have not occurred previously. When the playing field changes, society looks to the law as the deciding factor. Therefore, attorneys may be deluged with work entailing Intellectual Property, Stockholders Rights, and Labor Law, to name but a few. The clock is ticking. There is little more than a month left before Congress demands an answer. So, it would behoove attorneys and the rest of us to put on our thinking caps, get our minds in gear, and put our collective brains to work! Perhaps, given a bit of good old-fashioned brainstorming, a workable long-term solution will emerge within the next month. Let's hope so.

Chapter 13

Opportunity Knocks for GM during the Decline of the Industrial Age

All around us, as far as the eye can see, the universe holds together, and only one way of considering it is really possible, that is, to take it as a whole, in one piece.
--Teilhard de Chardin, *Le Phenomene Humain*[64]

In this chapter, we will address the serious threat to survival facing General Motors. For those who may have been in a coma or lost in some "dead zone" of the world for most of 2008 and 2009, let us summarize how GM has found itself on tenterhooks with a limited window of time to turn itself around. Liabilities exceed Assets by a factor of two to one, Shareholders' Equity continues to plunge deeper into the red, and a government deadline looms over the firm. These and related problems laden a corporate leadership that passively attempted to, as GM Chairman Rick Wagoner said, "Hang on as long as we can." However, the time has come and gone for Wagoner and his crew to do their job or get off the pot!

General Motors, incorporated under the state laws of Delaware, aka the "Great State of du Pont," remains subject to corporate and other pertinent laws of the United States. As a U.S. corporation, GM exists as a legal person—an artificial creature of the law. Because of this status, the corporation exists merely as a shell that can own assets, enter into contracts, and sue and be sued. In addition, GM can engage in a host of other structures, conducts, and performances allowed to this kind of legal entity. However, we must note that GM, or any other corporate entity, is neither sacred nor evil, neither generous nor greedy, neither responsible nor malfeasant. Any human characteristics conjured up and projected by pundits and the public should be attributed to the decision-makers acting behind the corporate veil—a veil that offers them, and shareholders, substantial degrees of protection. Alternately, the same corporate laws providing this protection to managers and board members simultaneously demand the fulfillment of specific fiduciary responsibilities.

Under the laws of incorporation developed within the context of the constitutional republic that we embrace as the United States, the principal responsibility of any corporate officer or director remains its fiduciary responsibility to its owners, the shareholders. Though protected by various legal constraints, any other real or perceived obligations to employees, the larger community, and other third parties remain secondary. Furthermore, even if a shareholder, such as I, Dr. Sase, or a colleague, may advocate for protection of workers, the environment, or other issues affecting one's kindred network and the larger community, the principal corporate directive remains a fiduciary responsibility of the board and officers to all of the shareholders. If the board and officers of a corporation place their own interests or the interests of employees and any other stakeholder before the interests of the shareholder, it violates this primary fiduciary duty.

Robbing from Peter to Pay Paul?

In his article in the *Detroit Free Press*,[65] Tim Higgins discussed the technically legal Pension Gambit of borrowing from Peter to pay Paul. Over the course of 2008, the pension fund was bled from a total of $20.0 billion to a negative balance of ($12.4) billion—a decrease of $34.4 billion. Overlooking the old adage of "If you borrow something from somebody without telling them, it's stealing," we at least must consider the somewhat covert draining of the pension fund as a loan--one that must be repaid. By its nature, a pension does not constitute a retractable gift or bonus to the recipient. Rather, a pension remains an obligation to pay for past services, deferred in respect to time of payment. This deferment benefits the corporate cash flow while delaying and usually reducing the tax obligation of the payee until his/her period of retirement.

From the viewpoint of the shareholder, this $34.4 billion "loan" represents an increase in Liabilities that, in turn, decreases Shareholder Equity. However, if General Motors Corporation cannot repay all or even a portion of this loan, retirees should be covered in part by the U.S. Government through the Pension Benefit Guaranty Corporation (PBGC). We should note that the PBGC is an independent agency of the United States government that was created by the Employee Retirement Income Security Act of 1974 (ERISA) to encourage the continuation and maintenance of voluntary private defined-benefit pension plans. Because the plan is financed from sources other than taxpayer dollars, any coverage provided by the PBGC does not directly affect taxpayers. However, because the PBGC remains, in effect, an insurance company funded by premiums from employers and a few other sources, concerns loom as to whether or not the PBGC can remain solvent throughout the present economic environment, given an escalating number of claims. So, ultimately, U.S. taxpayers could get stuck with the bill.

Before gaining public notoriety for this so-called loan, one unapproved by present and future retirees, the officers of General Motors successfully obtained a bridge loan during the waning days of the Bush administration. Thus far, this loan amounts to $13.4 billion. Given their performance projections for 2009 and beyond, GM officials returned to Washington to request an additional $16.6 billion. With this plea, the corporation soon ended up owing U.S. taxpayers a total of $30.0 billion in either cash or (cough) new equity. Assuming that the corporate profit forecast bears fruit in 2010, General Motors foresaw that it could commence a turnaround by that time. However, according to General Motors Corporation, Form 10-K (5 March 2009), "In connection with the preparation of our consolidated financial statements for the year ended December 31, 2008, we concluded that there was substantial doubt about our ability to continue as a going concern and our independent auditors included a statement in their audit report related to the existence of substantial doubt about our ability to continue as a going concern."

Following this path to possible ruination, some observers point to the Reagan era of rampant deregulation in the early 1980s, one that followed on the heels of stagflation (high unemployment along with high inflation) as the beginning of the end. Others point to the death of former GM President Ed Cole in 1977—in a plane crash that many of my elders contended was not accidental-- as the effective starting point of the regime responsible for the current donnybrook. However, more observers point to the decision against DuPont,[66] in which the Federal Court held that the acquisition of 23% of General Motors common stock by the DuPont Company had insulated them from free competition in most of the GM market for automobile finishes and fabrics. This tended to create a monopoly of a line of commerce (in violation of § 7 of the Clayton Act) as the crossroads. However, let us focus our analysis on the financial statements of the last five years in order to comprehend the deterioration of our still-affluent industrial society.

Sometimes we are tempted to trample this super-abundance back into the matter from which it sprang without stopping to think how impossible and monstrous such an act against nature would be.

--Teilhard de Chardin, ibid.

From the shareholders' point of view, the decline of their Equity position in GM, the probability of its recovery, and the duration of this recovery remain critical concerns. The decline in Equity follows a historical measure. Using 2004 as the start date, we find that Shareholder Equity has decreased at an increasing rate, from a high of $27.4 billion to a low of negative ($86.2) billion by the end of 2008. To date, this decline equals $113.6 billion lost over five years. Continuing along the same path, the Equity may decline to a negative ($143.0) billion by the end of 2009. For a more conservative estimate, we could include only the burn-through of the additional $16.6 billion requested in Federal loans. In contrast, this would plunge the Equity to a negative ($111.7) billion.

What does this mean? It means that General Motors faces the difficult, if not impossible, task of restoring shareholder value. Fairly simple and transparent math supports this assertion. If General Motors performs at the average of the positive earnings of its recent past and retains all of its net income within the business in order to rebuild Equity to the break-even point (meaning that the Equity Value per Share would equal $0.00), it will take many years. How long, you ask? Let's do a few simple calculations.

First, take the Equity of negative ($82.2) billion (31 December 2008) and subtract the additional $25.5 billion in Federal loans received, as well as requested, through 2009 (note that GM also borrowed funds from additional sources). Assuming only the burn-through of cash from U.S. taxpayers, the Shareholders Equity would fall to a negative ($111.7) billion. Next, let us take the corporate earnings from 1998 through 2004, the years that produced a positive Net Income annually for the firm. If first we correct the earnings from these years for inflation to 2008 dollars and then calculate the average of these adjusted values, we might expect General Motors to sustain average earnings of $3.9 billion per annum in today's dollars. However, we should remember that GM has shrunk considerably in both size and market share since 2004. Therefore, a figure of $3.9 billion per year seems potentially over-optimistic. Nevertheless, if we must err, let us err on the conservative side. This means that corporate losses have been so extreme that it will take until the year 2039 to move Equity Value per Share above $0.00. I don't know about you, but I, Dr. Sase, will be eighty-nine years old by then, God willing. Even if GM does not draw on the additional $16.6 billion of Federal funds, it will take until 2034 for shareholders to break even.

Over the past five years, the value of corporate Assets have fallen more than 80%, from $482 billion to $91 billion. Unfortunately, Liabilities have not fallen as much. At the end of 2004, Assets exceeded Liabilities by 6%. However, Assets had fallen to a mere 51% of Liabilities by the end of 2008. To put the decline into a long-term perspective, this deterioration of the balance sheet has occurred during the last fifth of a 25% drop in market share that began in the early 1980s. This downward spiral now leaves the company with a total market share of less than 22%. Though management has changed and tweaked its business model in recent years, it fails to work. As in the George Lucas film *Stars Wars, Episode I*, the "Galactic Senate" has voiced a motion of no confidence for a leadership that merely treads water. What to do? What to do?

"Shut It Down and Throw the Bums Out!"
Though numerous talking heads have expressed their views in a genteel manner, other voices have spoken more bluntly and to the point. Regardless of their demeanor, members of the "Galactic Senate" agree that the situation must be resolved without further delay. Regardless of what form the company currently takes, through the actions of the Federal government, American taxpayers now constitute a major block of GM stakeholders. Can we collectively

muster a set of tools that emulates that of bank-restructuring powers exercised by our Federal government? If so, we should move quickly to drain the auto-industry quagmire. We should do so in the same way that one would move to restructure a failing financial institution for which collapse certainly would carry widespread negative externalities for society at large. Therefore, under such a restructuring plan, the Federal government and GM shareholders could have worked in concert to shut down the operation of General Motors for thirty days, dismiss the current management team, and salvage those components of the business that hold the greatest probability of survival. From out of the ashes, a viable company may have emerged.

Avoiding the "B" Word

As this alternate approach to solving this critical problem proved legally, politically, and economically feasible, it could have allowed General Motors to avoid market-melting bankruptcy proceedings. Even as the course of events dictated that GM must enter into Chapter Eleven bankruptcy (rehabilitation or reorganization), or, in lieu of success in this attempt, Chapter Seven bankruptcy (basic liquidation), the same issues outlined below will apply.

Relying upon sound economic principles and on the information that we hear repeatedly from many sources, the probability that most of the GM corporate elements can survive intact appears low. Within the context of domestic and global market fragmentation, even a resolution of the current credit crisis may not permit the recovery of sales that would allow General Motors to regain a market share to support the technical and managerial overhead that it continues to carry. Furthermore, the minimal differentiation of some models marketed under the nameplates of several makes continues an atmosphere of redundancy and duplication of costs.

Due to the long-term shrinkage of GM market share, many observers have and continue to harbor serious doubts as to the viability of the numerous product lines and the continued support of a large tech center and other fixed corporate elements. Many retain an affection for certain makes and models that we would hate to see vanish. However, we must put aside these emotions in the light of the cold reality that threatens the current survival of the entire automotive industry. Therefore, extreme conditions may demand radical changes. As in a game of cards, a business in such a precarious situation must lead with its strongest suit.

A detailed examination of market share and relative strengths will lead us to the obvious decisions. Let's start with GM's product line. Though Pontiac, Buick, and Saturn provide a similar lineup of products, Chevrolet alone currently contributes 60% to the corporate market share. In contrast, these other three makes contribute only a fifth of this share. Can a surviving corporate configuration continue to support three secondary brands as individual entities? If not, the options for action must include the following: 1) Sell the three smaller brands to other producers, assuming that a viable purchaser steps forward. 2) Fold their productive capacity into Chevrolet to create one strong survivor, though we must recognize that the resulting excess capacity would constitute a costly burden at this time. 3) Shut them down. However, recent episodes suggest that this option may prove too costly and lengthy for the near term.

Regardless of the fate of these other makes, establishing Chevrolet as a new, stand-alone entity would take it off the books of General Motors Corporation. If the latter files for bankruptcy protection, Chevrolet would be shielded from much of the market stigma affecting GM. Such a separation would enable Chevrolet to rebuild itself as a stronger national and global brand.

Next on the agenda, we must consider the future of GMC and Cadillac. In respect to GMC, the possibilities include reforming it into a separate truck company or integrating it with Chevy truck production as one make. The situation of Cadillac gleams more uniquely. A general consensus seems to have developed that Cadillac should continue intact. Though the make contributes only 1.2% to the corporate market share, continued production of a luxury line remains a valuable card to play in the market (as Chrysler demonstrated backhandedly when it dropped its Imperial brand). Furthermore, Cadillac represents one of the few GM brands to have gained market share during the last eight years. However, the drawbacks come in the form of potential cost impediments from a lack of economies of scale. These may make it difficult for Cadillac to survive as a stand-alone company.

Finally, we must question the future of the remaining pieces of GM. Hummer has enjoyed a narrow niche market that satisfies a real need for specialty construction-industry and government vehicles. Due to its current stakeholder status, the intent of the Federal government with respect to this product line must be considered. On the other hand, Saab and Opel provide an intellectual property (IP) link to small-vehicle technology as well as direct access to the European market. Though either of these two makes could stand conceivably as brands on their own, maintaining ties to both companies through shared IP could prove cost effective for a surviving core U.S. company.

These possibilities address the imperative need for immediate action to either fix or scrap General Motors. However, the feasibility and potential success of such sweeping plans pose considerable legal, political, and economic challenges. It seems that we can develop some creative ways to effect positive change while avoiding the negative after-effect of bankruptcy proceedings. If not, General Motors and other firms will have to muddle through the bankruptcy process.

"You Can Never Solve a Problem on the Level on Which It Was Created."

– Albert Einstein

Specifically, what can economists and other readers do to facilitate this problem-solving process? The simple answer resonates as "Think outside the box." However, to leave the reader with this "hackney expression" seems simpering. Therefore, let us turn over the forum to greater minds that may stimulate us on the road to creativity. First, let's hear from American scientist Linus Pauling, who was awarded the Nobel Peace Prize for his campaign against above-ground nuclear testing. Pauling stated, "The best way to get a good idea is to get a lot of ideas." Next, let's give the floor to Albert Einstein, Nobel Prize winner in Physics, who was named Person of the Century by *Time* magazine. Einstein reminded us, "The intuitive mind is a sacred gift and the rational mind is a faithful servant. We have created a society that honors the servant and has forgotten the gift."

On the lighter side, American humorist Will Rogers asked this question toward the end of the Hoover administration: "If stupidity got us into this mess, then why can't it get us out?" To this, American photographic pioneer Edwin Land might respond "Creativity is the sudden cessation of stupidity."

Turning to the pragmatic foundations of creativity, German psychoanalyst Erich Fromm tells us, "Creativity requires the courage to let go of certainties." German philosopher Friedrich Nietzche states poetically that you "need chaos in your soul to give birth to a dancing star." More technically, French philosopher and scientist Rene Descartes instructs us to "divide each difficulty into as many parts as is feasible and necessary to resolve it." Of course, there is no guarantee that any proposed solution will work; that's life. Therefore, let us recall the words of the American science fiction writer Ray Bradbury, who proposed that life is "trying things to see if they work."

Hopefully, these words and the thoughts behind them will help to stimulate inspired creative genius in order to help General Motors in its time of need. Therefore, in closing, we share a favorite reflection on creativity and genius by pioneering American psychologist and philosopher William James, who said "Genius means little more than the faculty of perceiving in an unhabitual way." Let's give the last word to gifted American musician and actor Oscar Levant: "There's a fine line between genius and insanity. I have erased this line."

Chapter 20

The Strange Case of General Motors' "Surgical" Bankruptcy

> "Switch on the box, Mr. Spock is on the table,
> Dr. McCoy is unable to connect his brain,
> Sweating and straining,
> Well, it seemed so simple at the time."

--"Never You Mind" by Semisonic, *Feeling Strangely Fine*[67]

Members of the White House Automotive Task Force spent the first part of April 2009 in meetings and on conference calls with General Motors officials and their advisers. On 12 April 2009, Micheline Maynard and Michael J. de la Merced of the New York Times introduced us to a new term—"surgical" bankruptcy--when they wrote that the "goal is to prepare for a fast 'surgical' bankruptcy, the people who had been briefed on the plans said. G.M., which had been granted $13.4 billion in federal aid, insists that a quick restructuring is necessary so its image and sales are not damaged permanently."[68] Could it be that this term heralds back to the battle between scalpels and chainsaws during the presidential debates of 2008?

The Past is Prelude

In the preceding chapter, we wrote that from the shareholders' point of view, the decline in their equity position, the probability of its recovery, and the duration of a possible recovery at General Motors remain critical concerns. Since 2004 GM Shareholder Equity decreased from a high of $27.4 billion to a negative low of ($86.2) billion at the end of 2008. To that date, this decline amounted to $113.6 billion over five years. As a conservative estimate including only the burn-through of the additional $16.6 billion in Federal loans, Equity may further plunge to ($111.7) billion in 2009.

In addition, we asked if a viable, surviving GM can continue to support multiple secondary brands of vehicles. If not, then the options for action must include the following: 1. Sell the three smaller brands to other producers, assuming that a viable purchaser steps forward. 2. Fold their productive capacity into Chevrolet to create one strong survivor, though we must recognize that the resulting excess capacity at this time would constitute a costly burden. 3. Shut them down, though recent episodes suggest that this option may prove too costly and lengthy for the near term. Over the past month, it appears that the opinions of a larger set of stakeholders, including the Federal Government, have paralleled our thoughts. This month, we will explore some of the recent developments that have been put on the table as well as add a few of our own.

Montgomery "Scotty" Scott: "A Few Seconds After They Sent This One Up Through the Transporter, That Duplicate Appeared. Except It's Not a Duplicate. It's an Opposite. Two of the Same Animal, But Different."

--"The Enemy Within" episode of *Star Trek,* 6 October 1966.

For those fans of Star Trek (whether they have grown into successful attorneys economists and others, or have remained residents in their parent's basement past the age of thirty), the present restructuring scheme laid on General Motors reminds one that Star Trek episode in which Captain James T. Kirk splits into the "Good Kirk" and the "Evil Kirk."

The White House Automotive Task Force announced that it opted to split GM into two companies in bankruptcy court. Restructured to survive, the court began to create a "Good GM," one with strong brands including Chevrolet and Cadillac. The court has saddled the other firm, the "Bad GM," with weaker brands like Saturn and Hummer to be sold off later during extended bankruptcy proceedings.

This idea has circulated swiftly through the media and has received further endorsement from GM's newly appointed interim chairman, Kent Kresa. Mr. Kresa, chairman emeritus of Northrop Grumman, widely has received credit for keeping that aerospace defense contractor afloat during its own bankruptcy proceedings. On 2 April 2009, Kresa told *Automotive News*[69] that if GM must to go into bankruptcy, splitting the company into two entities would be "a great idea." Kresna himself floated the idea that if the company must enter Chapter 11 bankruptcy, it could split into a "good GM" and a "bad GM." Such a plan would help the "good GM" to quickly emerge as a viable company. Kresna maintains that the concept presents a "wonderful idea for allowing a new General Motors to emerge."

However, Kresa has forewarned that this reorganization technique "has its problems, and all of our people are looking at it very hard." He adds that "There are a lot of constituents right now that have some dibs on the assets...."

The bankruptcy has to deal with each of those and make sure that whatever comes out is reasonable. This is not a done deal. We want to do something that would be done quickly." We must note that as non-executive chairman Kent Kresa has stated that he has not personally involved himself in any of the negotiations with the UAW or with the bondholders.

363 – The Number of the Beast?
Probably not. However, on 2 April 2009 Frank Langfitt of *All Things Considered*[70] discussed that the Obama administration has explored Section 363 within Chapter 11 of the bankruptcy code.

Section 363 often provides a key element of the bankruptcy process in respect to the sale of assets. Under Section 363(f), a bankruptcy trustee or debtor-in-possession, in this case "parent GM," may sell the bankruptcy estate's assets, in this case "good GM," free and clear of any interest in such property. This "free and clear" provision provides a means for the debtor to consummate the sale quickly as competing interests in the property do not require resolution.

However, when the corporate parent remains the debtor in bankruptcy, Section 363 also considers the shares of the debtor's subsidiaries as "assets" that may be sold. As a caveat, attorneys Lisa Jack and George W. Shuster, Jr. of the Wilmer Hale firm (wilmerhale.com) offer a recent example from the U.S. Bankruptcy Court for the District of Delaware. The authors recount the case of Insilco Technologies that provides a cautionary reminder to buyers that "a stock sale is still a stock sale, and that a buyer who takes the shares of a corporation under a 363 order will still be responsible for the subsidiary's indebtedness."[71]

Prior to filing for bankruptcy, Insilco closed a deal with Amphenol Corporation to sell Insilco's subsidiaries as well as all of the stock in its wholly owned subsidiary, Precision Cable Mfg. Co., Inc. (PCM). Two years after the sale the liquidating trustee filed a preference action for more than $1 million against PCM that had become a subsidiary of Amphenol Corporation. Though both the co-debtor assets and the PCM *stock* had been sold free and clear of interests, PCM's *assets* had not. Jack and Schuster explain that "As PCM's assets were not transferred under the Sale Order, that order did not enjoin the pursuit of claims or interests against PCM or its assets."

The obvious but critical point surfaces that a stock sale of a non-debtor subsidiary "free and clear" offers very limited protection to the buyer. In buying a corporation—not merely its assets—a buyer does not receive any discharge or protection from the corporation's indebtedness under Section 363."[72]

Rebirth of Old Plans
Sprinkled throughout the preceding chapters, I have sketched some of the events, and plans that emerged from these events, in the mid-1950s. The approximate time frame extended from 1954, the year after Charles E. Wilson

divested himself of his holdings in General Motors to avoid potential conflicts of interest in his new position with the President Eisenhower administration as Secretary of Defense and the Court's decision in the case of the United States v. Du Pont & Co., 353 U.S. 586 (1957), that required DuPont to divest itself of GM shares in order to preserve its paint supplier contract with GM. Apart from research in recent years in an attempt to verify names, dates, and facts, my knowledge of the situation stems from my entrenchment in it as an eyewitness for a few years as well as my understanding of parents' appraisal reflected in their simple, clear explanation.

In essence (or *aessence* as some of us prefer), this series of events enabled interested parties from the first generation of GM wealth to align a group of children to which they could pass a significant amount of the then eighty-eight million General Motors shares. Furthermore, they identified and imposed an executive hierarchy among these children based upon discussions of kindred networks, cousinages, bloodlines, and other concepts which may appear as arcane to many people today. With powers and rights that ostensibly flow from the percentage of total corporate shares passed through trust accounts, these dowagers secured the hierarchy and held it in reserve. (However, many "tribal elders" pointed out that this transfer was set up as a tax dodge—an assertion that has gained strength in recent years.)

Nevertheless, the original "estate" created through the contribution of holdings amounted to approximately 28% of total outstanding GM shares at that time. In addition, toward the end of the above-cited time frame, a different faction added another 12% of holdings, bringing the total to around 40%. To my knowledge, no further additions entered into this estate that was structured into some kind of elaborate dynasty (generation-skipping) trust.

The mammoth drop in the value of shareholder equity at GM to a negative ($112) billion in 2009 created a game changer. Though the market-price of shares has been bouncing slightly above the par value of $1.67 for the month preceding the stocks delisting from the exchanges, the equity value of the shares remained at zero, with no dividend paid. Therefore, any bid-price at this level only reflects market speculation in respect to possible future value and earnings and courtroom turnarounds. As a result, if this 1950s estate continues to exist intact, it possesses no real equity value. Furthermore, it appears to have been structured so that over the past five decades, the dividends flowed to the contributors to the trust and their direct heirs. In effect, the block of GM stock never increased and has now fallen worthless. How do I know this? Between the ages of four and eight, I was present and made party to the scheme along with a couple of dozen other lads my own age.

For the sake of discussion, let us assume that this estate remains intact and that the members of the above-mentioned group of children (or the successors of those who have not survived) may step forward, though thus far we have seen no one rushing to claim control of "bad GM." However, the "good GM" may present very different attractions. Therefore, the following proposal rests upon the assumptions that members of this group 1) remain willing, 2) that they have adequate knowledge, skills, and life experience for the task, and 3) that the estate described remains legally protected.

One proposal calls for the transfer/leveraged sale of the "good GM" to this group that, in a fashion, remains tied to equity that currently possesses zero value. Handing over the reins of "good GM" over to these equity holders would resolve the age-old owner-agent problem. When an owner and a manager (agent) are in fact the same person, the potential conflicts that would otherwise arise from differences in interests, motivations, and loyalties simply go away.

Though we could debate the finer points of the owner-agent problem until the cows come home, let us proceed to the more essential points of this proposal. In order to ensure the financial feasibility of a "good GM," we propose placing a cap on executive compensation. This cap would amount to earnings of seven times the average wage/salary of all employees. For example, if the average earnings at the company equal $90 thousand per year, the cap sets at $630 thousand. Granted, to many people this may seem like an enormous amount, especially given that that the President of the United States earns a salary of only $400 thousand per annum (though he does receive expense accounts amounting to $159 thousand gets to live for free in a "really swell house"). However, in respect to recent GM total earnings of more than $14 million per year paid to Rick Wagoner, this cap appears relatively small to those that understand the 24/7 responsibility that owner-agents must assume.

On the flip side of the coin, we must remember that, collectively, this owner-agent group would maintain a claim to a substantial portion of total corporate shares. However, any financial arrangement of dubious value would not offer suitable enticement or motivation. In other words, one should not expect this group to pay off the $112+ billion debt incurred by failed past management while accepting a limit on their own potential future income.

Therefore, we would need to condition this proposal in such a way that any restructuring to create a "good GM" must include a transfer of assets and liabilities that produces shareholder equity in the new company of at least zero. Subsequently, any increase in owner-agent equity must result from measurable performance.

This zero-value baseline may prove problematic on many fronts due to the demands imposed by the large number of outside investors who hold a substantial number of shares. Alternately, structuring a "good GM" so that the baseline value of equity per share stands at its par value of $1.67 per share—an amount that approximates the ending market price before delisting—would help to sustain public confidence in the company as well as avoid setting any undesirable precedents in this present economic climate. At par, the current 566 million shares are worth $945.2 million. Of course, we should acknowledge the possible necessity of splitting the shares between the "good" and the "bad" GMs.

Cutting the Cake

During this "surgical" removal of "Spock's Brain," we expect the Federal Government to act in the role of an interim partner (debt holder and temporary shareholder). It appears that both private and public sector interests harbor the hope that this relationship endure for as short a period as possible. As implied above, the consummation of the deal work may require that the Federal Government (i.e. the American taxpayer) convert some of its debt holdings into shares of stock with the stated goal that the surviving company will repurchase these shares as rapidly as possible. Such a plan would ensure a timely severance of dependency by the business from the government as well as dismiss any voting rights that the government may exercise in this private venture.

In respect to the owner-agent group, no one definitively had resolved the matter of share distribution in the 1950s as the estate passed to the titular stewardship of one participant through the signing of stacks of papers in the settlement. Though partitioning the estate into smaller blocks may stimulate jubilation among some individuals, such a division would defeat the original purpose of assembling this voting-block. To the best of my knowledge, concerned parties have not openly revisited or resolved this matter as the dormant nature of the estate (not to mention its present loss of value) has left this point moot.

However, in recent decades the Limited Liability Company (LLC) has emerged as a business form that may provide the means to allow for simultaneous control and disbursement of holdings. Chiefly inspired by the GmbH, a type of business organization in Germany, the LLC offers us a newer business structure allowed by state statute. In the U.S., the first Limited Liability Company appeared in Wyoming in 1977 as special interest legislation for an oil firm.

Due to uncertainty over the tax treatment of LLCs, this new business form developed slowly throughout the 1980s. However, in 1988 the Internal Revenue Service issued a ruling stating that it would treat any Wyoming-style LLC as a partnership for tax purposes. That opened the flood gates. So, by 1996 virtually every state had passed LLC legislation and the National Conference of Commissioners on Uniform State Laws adopted the Uniform Limited Liability Company act in 1996, (later revised in 2006).

In respect to the mysterious 40% block of GM equity, referred to above as the estate that continues to exist at least as urban legend, the LLC may provide the suitable vehicle for carrying the matter. If we envision an LLC as a club with two kinds of members, managing and regular, then we have the working model for this proposal. Conceptually, the proposal appears fairly simple. Turn the estate into an LLC. Then, distribute LLC membership shares among the original group of owner-agents (or their rightful successors) selected under the 1955 plan.

Such an arrangement would allow the LLC member shares to increase, decrease, or be exchanged under a set of by-laws, to be established. Also, this plan would leave intact the underlying corporate shares as a unified estate. Of course, further details would need to be developed among the group of owner-agents with the assistance of attorneys practiced in this area of law.

Plan B—Yes, There is One

Our Plan B provides a course that is much in concept, but more complex in execution. If all interested parties cannot survive emergent from Chapter 11 reorganization, then let General Motors proceed into Chapter 7 bankruptcy. The question arises as to who would get which assets? For clarification of the process for those of us who are less familiar with Chapter 7 of Title 11 of the United State Code (Bankruptcy Code), let us refer to GM's Restated Certificate of Incorporation that states "In the event of the liquidation, dissolution or winding up of the Corporation, whether voluntary or involuntary, after there shall have been paid or set apart for the holders of Preferred Stock and Preference Stock the full preferential amounts to which they are entitled, the holders of Common Stock shall be entitled to receive the assets of the Corporation remaining for distribution to its stockholders ratably on a per share basis."[73]

What this means is that under normal circumstances, debt holders stand first in line, preferred stock holders receive second claim on any remaining assets, and common stockholders take what assets remain, if any. However, a review of the 31 December 2008 Consolidated Balance Sheets reveals that of the 6,000,000 authorized shares of GM Preferred Stock none is issued and outstanding.

What happened to GM's Preferred Stock? The answer dates back to a 1993 preferred stock redemption by the corporation. On 2 March 1993, directors of the General Motors Corporation authorized the company to redeem two longtime preferred stock issues in a move that cost about $265 million and created windfall profits for holders. The press release stated that "G.M. plans to redeem all $5.00 series and $3.75 series shares, issued in 1930 and 1946 respectively, on May 1." The board stated that redeeming the two issues eliminated "antiquated covenants" which required General Motors to hold excess cash to pay dividends. (Note: If a company fails to pay a dividend on non-voting Preferred Stock, the holders of those shares acquire voting rights.) These issues were repurchased at prices double the previous day's closing price on the New York Stock Exchange.[74]

Therefore, as of entrance into Chapter 11 proceedings in 2009 no preferred shares existed outside of the corporate treasury. This means that common stockholders stand in line second to debt holders. However, an interesting development came to the forefront. On 27 March 2009, General Motors Corporation offered to convert half of a $20 billion funding obligation to a union-aligned retiree healthcare trust into preferred stock. According to a CNBC[75] report, "GM offered the United Auto Workers union $10 billion in cash, amortized over 20 years, and $10 billion of preferred stock with a 9 percent coupon, to fund the healthcare trust."

Depending on what may materialize over the next couple of years, The UAW may find itself in a position to lay claim to the remaining real estate--the plants and affixed equipment. Potentially, this could place labor in the role of entrepreneur in forming yet another new automotive firm out of the ashes of the old ones. Indeed, this would produce a noodle-bending conundrum for attorneys who have previously set on opposite sides of the bargaining table.

And That's All I Have to Say About That.—Forrest Gump.

Chapter 21

The Rape of General Motors:
Bicycles, Bloodsuckers, Lizards, and Werewolves

"A great civilization is not conquered from without until it has destroyed itself from within."

-- Will Durant, American Writer, Historian, and Philosopher

"Companies go out of business. People don't!"
--Steve Carrell, as Michael G. Scott in *The Office*[76]

Jimmy had a bicycle. He built it himself. He entered his bicycle in races and won a great deal of prize money for many years. Then one day, Chuck came along. He told Jimmy, "I can ride longer and faster than you can, but I have no bike of my own." So Chuck suggested a deal by which he would ride Jimmy's bike in races. When Chuck won, he would give Jimmy a portion of the winnings. In addition, Chuck promised to keep the bike in good repair. Jimmy agreed and became Chuck's silent partner in this new venture.

This arrangement worked very well for a number of years while there were only a few strong contestants in the races. However, over time, more and more young, strong bicyclists entered the competitions, which they began to win. Chuck also continued to win, though not as much each time and not as often. Eventually, he found ways of increasing his own share of the winnings while continuing to pay Jimmy his fair share. Chuck skimped on the maintenance of the bike. At first, the decreases in the upkeep did not show as Chuck reaped a modest "bonus" from his actions. However, towards the end of his racing career, the defects became increasingly apparent and the value of the bike decreased.

As Chuck intended to retire from racing and grow asparagus, the long-term condition of the bicycle mattered less and less to him while he managed to pocket a greater percentage of the winnings. During his last couple of races, Chuck won nothing, so Jimmy received nothing. In the last race, Chuck ran the bike into the ground and it fell apart. After giving back the worthless wreck to Jimmy, Chuck walked away with money in his pocket. The End.

General Motors Is Dead. Long Live "Federal Motors"!

Like it or not, the Federal Government, and hence the American taxpayer, owns controlling interest in the new beast that is General Motors, whatever its *nom de jour*. However, the Obama administration has stated that it has no intention of managing the company itself. It has left this formidable task to the "best and brightest" of manufacturing, the same breed of MBAs using the same ineffectual "business models" that dragged the industry to its knees over the past couple of decades.

GM Interim CEO Fritz Henderson dragged out the same old tired rhetoric that has been foisted on the American public numerous times. In a press conference, he said that the company "will create a leaner, quicker, more customer and completely product-focused company, one that's more cost competitive and has a competitive balance sheet."[77] This quote amounts to nothing more than a collection of buzzwords that were bouncing around in MBA courses thirty years ago. Nothing new here! On the other hand, whatever management team takes the helm of GM must maintain its fiduciary responsibility to shareholders. This group of stockholders includes the U.S. Federal Government at 60%, the Canadian Government at 12.5%, the United Auto Workers at 17.5%, and unsecured bondholders at 10%. Previous stockholders get zilch.

Wall Street Redux

The share of General Motors that GM-UAW gets, a swap of cash for stock, is 17.5%. Car Czar Steve Rattner, head of the Presidential Task Force on the Auto Industry, is demanding that the bankruptcy court simply wipe away the money that GM owes workers for their retirement health insurance and replace it with stock in the New GM. Whether intentional or not, this move effectively splits the union in two. Divide and conquer?

This deal splits the equity interests of older workers against the wage interests of younger workers. In order to guarantee pension and medical benefits for retirees, the stock must be valuable. Also, management has a primary fiduciary responsibility to shareholders. To gain value, the New GM must minimize costs. To minimize costs, it must produce with as low a cost of labor as possible. To maximize the value for older workers, earnings and benefits to younger workers must be minimized. This would be done either by suppressing U.S. wages or by moving production to China, India, and other locations. Incidentally, these countries are enjoying the growth of sustainable markets along with less regulation and cheaper labor. Recently, Chinese car-buyers have gone on waiting lists for back-ordered vehicles.

Under corporate law, an investor spins the wheel and takes his/her chances. Normally, shareholder voices on the board of directors reduce the risk. However, in the case of GM, that check-and-balance has deteriorated in recent decades. Upper management loaded the board with their own cronies and "yes men" as that same management led the corporation down the road to ruin while lining their own pockets. The time has arisen for shareholders of Old GM to cry foul. This situation is tantamount to highway robbery on the Autobahn or piracy on the High Seas of Finance. We suggest that our readers watch Oliver Stone's film *Wall Street*[78] in order to refresh their memories as to how such nefariousness can occur as well as its results. In fact, a sequel to the movie is planned with Michael Douglas reprising his role as Corporate Lizard Gordon Gekko. Art imitates life? You be the judge.

New Lamps for Old
What happened to the shareholders of Old GM? They have been left with nothing. The cavalier attitude of the Task Force for the Auto Industry seems to be "You play the game and take your chances." However, is this really the best approach? Furthermore, was the game rigged by members of the financial industry from which leading members of the Task Force came?

Corporations have three types of shareholders. The first is the short-term investor who is involved in frequent in-and-out trading. They are playing the Wall Street game by buying low to sell high. The second kind of investor is represented by the person or organization that seeks to maintain and grow their wealth over a long period of time. They engage in the buy-and-hold strategy that Rattner's former (?) Wall Street colleagues hate. Buy-and-hold trading does not generate commissions--in-and-out trades do.

The third genre of shareholders engages in what economists and others refer to as *stewardship of wealth*. Generally, this involves large blocks of stock that have been consolidated and transferred over multiple generations. Though some stewards may draw an income from these holdings, the predominant philosophy over the past fifty years has been one of "Do not touch a penny of it," as the purpose of the stewardship addresses other critical issues.

Essentially, the stewards remain part of, and tied to, large kindred networks that have held employment in the companies for a number of generations. These major stewardship blocks have provided leverage to insure that members of these extended families have jobs. These jobs have included not only rank-and-file production employment, but staff employment in engineering, accounting, finance, and other functional areas as well. However, a few major blocks of GM stock have become worthless overnight. The leverage used to help protect employment opportunities at General Motors has vanished in one fell swoop. This responsibility, once held by these stock stewards, now has shifted inadvertently to the U.S. Government. Good luck to it!

If the U.S. Government (taxpayers) hopes to recover its investment, it must sell its 60% interest for at least as much as it has, and will, put into the firm. To achieve this, the share-price bid in the financial market must prove adequate in order to meet this goal.

The assets must exceed the liabilities substantially. For this to happen, the firm must earn a profit in an increasingly competitive market while sustaining a smaller market share and volume of production. In order to make this happen, they must minimize their costs.

Who will purchase this stock? Currently, institutional investors, mutual funds, investment banks, and the like, buy and sell 90% of stock in the markets. Given the simple mechanics of supply and demand, dumping the government's 60% share of GM into the market merely would drive down the market price. Therefore, we can expect a handful of institutional investors to step forward and work out a deal with their former colleague, Steve Rattner.

Putting the "Rat" in Rattner

Steve Rattner co-founded Quadrangle Group LLC, a New York-based private-equity firm that invests in media companies and distressed debt. According to his disclosure forms, Quadrangle paid Rattner $3.1 million.

In order to avoid conflicts of interest, Rattner sold reported holdings of between $500,000 and $1 million that he held in Cerberus Institutional Partners LP Series 2, a fund managed by Cerberus Capital Management LP that holds Chrysler LLC. He also owned at least $105 million in various Quadrangle investments and reported holdings of between $500,000 and $1 million in Goldman Sachs Group Inc. As an interesting note, Rattner received more than $5,000 from Spencer Stuart, the closely held executive search firm that GM Interim Chairman Kent Kresa hired to find new directors for the GM board.

On 27 May 2009, journalists Jonathan D. Salant and Justin Blum of Bloomberg.com laid out the life and times of Steve Rattner quite well. In "Rattner Worth at Least $188 Million, Disclosures Show (Update Two)," they informed us that Rattner, who is portrayed as one of the common folk, now owns an airplane, used in an air-charter business, that is valued between $5 million and $25 million, and a horse farm in North Salem, New York, that is valued at between $5 million and $25 million. He held shares in an investment fund run by the majority owner of Chrysler LLC. In addition, Rattner sold guarantees of as much as $15 million on a credit-default swaps index tied to the secured debt of 100 companies, including the senior secured loans of General Motors. After three days, fresh fish only remains desirable to cats on the street.

The Old Bait and Switch?

If we look at the history of Sweden over the last half century, it will warn us of the potential hazards that come with nationalizing an industry—in this case, the lumber industry, which is critical to the Swedish economy. In this experience, the cost overruns and labor problems increased. However, management positioned from the ranks of government continued to have the same fiduciary responsibility to shareholders. This nationalization did not work well. Finally, the government returned the lumber industry to private ownership and control. After this experience, Sweden reversed its plans to nationalize its auto and aerospace industries.

To return the auto companies to private ownership, stock shares must appeal to investors. How can "Federal Motors" (or Government Motors as some have nicknamed it) reach this financial goal? By keeping production in the U.S. just long enough for the stock to be absorbed into Wall Street and then switch to China--bait and switch, just like selling a used car. From a cost standpoint, it would make sense to keep low-paying final assembly jobs in the U.S. to prepare imported cars-from-kits for our domestic market. However, many observers see a low incentive to keep engineering, technical, design, and similar jobs in the U.S. Any job that can be done on computer over the Internet will gravitate to the provider that presents the lowest cost. All that the New GM needs to remain a U.S. corporation is a "front office" in this country.

Who's being "Shanghaied"? Us!
On 19 May 2009, Ralph Nader reported to Allan Sloan of CNNMoney.com that he has grave concerns about the effect that the restructuring of GM may have on U.S. workers, consumers, investors, dealers, and communities.[79] Furthermore, Nader asks this question: do we want a U.S. industry or U.S. auto companies—meaning an industry with foreign ownership siphoning off the profits or domestic companies producing offshore? The New GM has expressed plans to increase the production of autos made in the U.S. to be sold in the U.S. However, Nader states that GM had revealed plans to begin selling Chinese-made vehicles in the U.S. in 2011.

Furthermore, Nader thinks that "GM is planning to reorganize around its Chinese operation and move as much of its U.S. production there as quickly as it can, eventually using Chinese-made vehicles to supply much of the U.S. market." On 28 May 2009, United Press International (UPI) released a statement that "President and Managing Director of GM China, Kevin Wale, said the business in China 'is run as separate joint ventures…in partnerships with Shanghai Automotive Group.' Michael Dunne, an industry analyst at J.D. Power and Associates China, said GM in China would remain 'insulated from the bankruptcy back home.'"

What are the true plans at "Federal Motors"? Perhaps the New GM plans on producing vehicles in kit form (remember Ford's Pinto kits sent abroad) shipped from China to be assembled by low-skilled, low-paid assemblers in the U.S. in order to fulfill their pledge to the American public.

In their subsequent treatise published in the *Wall Street Journal* on 29 May 2009, Ralph Nader and Robert Weissman stated this belief: rather than a "small, largely unaccountable, ad hoc task force made up of a handful of Wall Street expatriots," Congress should decide the fate of General Motors. In a restatement of points made in their letter of 18 May 2009 to Senator Chris Dodd and Congressman Barney Frank, they address ten pressing issues that should be answered to the satisfaction of the American people. In summary, these include a quest for cost-benefit analyses relating to plant shutdowns and dealership closures, clarification of issues involving tangled relationships with Chinese partners, rights of owner-shareholders to decide whether they want their company dissolved, and guarantees to taxpayer investment. Nader and Weissman ask, "Would a government-driven bankruptcy process comport with the rights of owner-shareholders?"

Cannibals Host the Bar-B-Q, and We're Invited!
Through "Car Czar" Rattner and his crew, the government has seized GM assets and has begun to divide them up among creditors. Documentary filmmaker Alex Jones and his posse of populists at Infowars tend to speak to the Average Joe on the street in their many expose films[80] and on their Web site. Because of the bold positions that they take, they stick their necks way out. In order to bolster their opinions, Jones and company do their dumpster-diving research very well. (In researching our article, we double checked their research in the *Wall Street Journal,* the *New York Times,* and other public sources.) In the Infowars.com Web posting of 3 June 2009, journalist Greg Palast wrote, "While GM workers are losing their retirement health benefits, their jobs, their life savings; while shareholders are getting zilch and many creditors getting hosed, a few privileged GM lenders--led by Morgan and Citibank--expect to get back 100% of their loans to GM, a stunning $6 billion. Citibank and Morgan, says Rattner, should get their whole enchilada--$6 billion right now."

Palast continues, "[I]s the forced bankruptcy of GM, the elimination of tens of thousands of jobs, just a collection action for favored financiers? Rattner was one of the privileged, select group of investors in Cerberus Capital, the owners of Chrysler. 'Owning' is a loose term. Cerberus 'owned' Chrysler the way a cannibal 'hosts' you for dinner. Cerberus paid nothing for Chrysler--indeed, they were paid billions by Germany's Daimler Corporation to haul it away. Cerberus kept the cash, then dumped Chrysler's bankrupt corpse on the US taxpayer."

Let's return to our story of Jimmy and Chuck. We feel that Jimmy should have hired a team of attorneys to go after Chuck before he ran Jimmy's bike into the ground. In the parallel universe of today's headlines, we feel that the stakeholders of General Motors, including labor of all strata as well as holders of defunct stock need a Van Helsing[81] leading a snarling pack of attorneys to run down the Werewolves of Wall Street and the Federally appointed Vampires who are sucking the blood out of the auto industry. If not, we may end up with "New World Motors."

Chapter 22

A Soiree on the River Styx:
Reflections on War--Redux

"On February 27, 1933, a mentally deranged Dutch Communist, Marinus van der Lubbe, lit a few small fires in the German parliament building, the Reichstag, in Berlin--not enough to set the building alight, but sufficient to get him hanged as the sole perpetrator afterward…. *Van der Lubbe…had bragged about intending to set the Reichstag on fire while having a beer in a pub. The Nazi SA, with ears everywhere, found out, and unbeknownst to van der Lubbe, an SA detachment entered the building through a disused central heating tunnel. While the Dutchman was busy lighting insignificant fires, using his shirt as tinder, the SA planted gasoline and incendiaries. Within minutes, the Reichstag was burning out of control."*
--Gregory Greene[82]

Why would the Nazis do this? In the preceding election, Hitler had been elected Prime Minister. However, he lacked majority control in both the government and the parliament. In the subsequent 5 March election, his party needed a decisive victory. Hitler's solution was to eliminate the Communist party and its 100 deputies. This feat would give the National Socialists the majority in the remaining parliament. By ensuring that the plan succeeded in destroying the Reichstag, Hitler could pronounce the fire to be a Communist conspiracy. Furthermore, by the next morning he had secured the signature of the aging President, von Hindenburg, on legislation that changed Germany from a democracy to a tyranny. The one hundred Communist deputies were arrested, civil rights were abrogated, and the country embraced Hitler as its Leader.

In war, truth is the first casualty.
– Aeschylus, Greek tragedian (525 BC – 456 BC)

When we first wrote the following piece, the Iraq War was in full swing during the waning days of the Bush Administration. This year, the war in Iraq continues while the original War on Terrorism has been reheated in Afghanistan. If one is "old enough" to remember, the original premise for going to war was predicated on the existence of "Weapons of Mass Destruction." As with a somewhat similar incident involving the battleship Maine as a prelude to the Spanish-American War, the unifying incident that banded us together in 2001 led to the emulative chant of "Remember 9/11."

The difference between the current war and the Spanish-American War is that we as a country got to watch live as a second plane crash into the World Trade Center and as the Twin Towers fell. In a pre-mass electronic media age, the story may have ended as the incident was enshrined in history. However, many educated researchers and journalist have refused to let the 9/11 story die. Architects, Engineers, and members of the construction industry have continued to challenge the official 9/11 stories and through their efforts, tangible evidence and analysis has emerged to further fuel the debate. Most recently, the medical community has implored us to consider the onslaught of cancer and other illnesses that are shortening the lives of the thousands of Americans who volunteered in the rescue efforts during the months following the collapse of the towers.

In the ongoing debate as to probable causes, negligence, and complicity involved with the 9/11 tragedy, extreme factions from the far right and the far left have fueled this debate to promote their own agendas. However, amidst the smoke and fury, we find a growing cadre of objective researchers using sound scientific method and publically available documents and data to calmly construct a case that we as a nation should at least review in a clear, detached manner. If we are to honor all of the victims of 9/11 who died, and continue to die, on the approaching eighth anniversary of this tragic event, we owe it to them and their surviving families to publically question how and why they sacrificed their lives. A few works for open minded men and women on both sides of the 9/11 debate include: 1) *CNN Tribute: America Remembers—The Events of September 11 and America's Response* (Cable News Network and Time Warner, 2002 edition, www.CNN.com/americaremembers). This DVD contains most of the published footage available at the time which is used by credible researchers as base data. 2) *911: In Plane Site: Directors Cut* (William Lewis and David von Kleist, Bridge Stone Media Group, 2006, www.inplanesite.org). This DVD is a touchstone for this field of research. It maintains a decent stance of objectivity while carefully constructing a well-produced analysis of the events of 9/11. 3) *911 Mysteries, Part 1: Demolitions* (911mysteries.com, 2008). This video remains available for free viewing at http://www.911weknow.com/911-mysteries-english/watch-911-mysteries-1-mainmenu-19). With the help of slow motion and annotations to the video images, the producers approach the subject using interviews, materials, and analyses garnered from architects, engineers, members of the demolition and allied industries. These experts represent the most credible witnesses in respect to many important issues surrounding the event.

Though none of these productions are perfect, they do present the neophyte explorer with a concise, but comprehensive review of the case over a course of four hours. We would suggest viewing them in the order listed. The CNN video gives the broad stroke overview of 9/11. Also, watching it for a second time with the audio turned off is recommended. *In Plane Site* considers the many facets of the story in that occurred in New York City, Washington, D.C. and rural Pennsylvania. Finally, *911 Mysteries* narrows the focus to the events in New York City and the analysis to the science and industries responsible for building and demolishing large structures. The second and third DVDs provide interested viewers with references to the more expansive cache of materials. However, remain objective and make up your own mind.

Reflections on War

Because of the interest that our piece on war generated last year, we decided to republish it for those who may have missed it. We constructed this column as inspired by, and in emulation of, the American author and satirist John Kendrick Bangs in his tome *A House-Boat on the Styx*.[83] Bangs was well known for creating a school of fantasy writing in which plots are set in the afterlife. We began to draw upon decades of thought and learning to bring this task to a head. Rather than pontificate our own views on the subject, we decided to draw upon the words of great minds. We thought, "What if we invited all of these personages to a cocktail party or parlor soiree?" Then, with a little bit of artistic license and help from our muse, we could allow them to discuss the matter with one another in their own words. So we decided to model the party on Bangs's third chapter, "[George] Washington Gives a Dinner." Original quotes from each celebrated guest are held within single quote marks in the body of the column.

***

Charon had busied himself all that morning and afternoon ferrying guests from the far side of the River Styx. Almost seventy years ago, he had arranged with General George Washington and members of the Houseboat Committee to use the houseboat on the Styx to host a soiree. Now he had arranged another soiree with Washington and the Committee. The houseboat, which resembled a Florentine barn set on top of a barge, was moored on the near side of the Styx in order to facilitate a special group of invitees who were coming from and returning to the Land of the Living.

All was prepared. The last of the guests had arrived. Charon stepped onto the houseboat to greet and address the guests. After a long day of work, first he decided to visit the little boatman's room to freshen himself. As he washed, Charon reflected on a verse from Ecclesiastes 3: 1-8 that a member of the Committee had posted on the mirror above the sink:

"For everything there is a season, and a time for every matter under heaven: A time to love and a time to hate, a time for war and a time for peace."

Finishing his toilette, Charon entered the grand parlor of the houseboat where the guests already had assembled and commenced to greet one another. With the exception of a few guests, the gathering quieted when Charon entered the room and walked up to the podium. Without hesitation, he began to speak:

"Ladies and gentlemen, I would like to welcome all of you to the first of these soirees since the one that we hosted on the eve of the Second World War in 1939. We decided to convene this meeting in the midst of what some of you know as the Global War on Terrorism and what others of you refer to as 'more of the same.' As you know, the present administration of the United States has proposed a 2009 federal budget. It includes 54% of its total as direct defense department allocation but continues a spending program in which two-thirds of federal expenditures have been identified as national defense by the U.S. government. What concerns us the most is not the present budget, but the fact that this spending pattern began well before the present administration. According to forecasts from many sources, this spending pattern and the horrors with which it is associated can be expected to continue well into the next decade unless a change in direction is taken."

Charon continued, "We have not convened this meeting of great minds to debate how or why this current war began any more than we are here to discuss how many persons most likely will gain from the continuation of these events, including myself, who holds the monopoly on trafficking across the Styx. Rather, we convened this meeting that we might lend some clarity, understanding, vision, and direction to those who are returning to the Land of the Living. We hope that they will carry our words with them to share amongst their fellow humans throughout the various nations of the earth."

"As the focus of this matter rests with his country and much of the current situation traces back to his presidency, I would like to call upon Ronald Reagan, former President of the United States to begin the discussion. Mr. President."

Reagan, who was slumbering at the head table, awoke, came forward, and said, "Thank you, Charon. To address the matter of war in general terms, I would like to put forth the thought that 'history teaches that war begins when governments believe the price of aggression is cheap.' With that thought, I turn the discussion over to Thomas Jefferson."

Jefferson stands and says, "Mr. Reagan, this is all well and good. However, I believe that you are missing the main point. Personally, 'I recoil with horror at the ferociousness of man. Will nations never devise a more rational umpire of differences than force? Are there no means of coercing injustice more gratifying to our nature than a waste of the blood of thousands and of the labor of millions of our fellow creatures?'"

Adjusting his loin cloth, Mahatma Gandhi rises and speaks: "I agree with Thomas and would carry this thought one step further. 'What difference does it make to the dead, the orphans and the homeless, whether the mad destruction is wrought under the name of totalitarianism or the holy name of liberty or democracy?'"

Twisting the ends of his mustache thoughtfully, Friedrich Nietzsche commented, "Thank you, Mahatma, for your wonderful words. What Mr. Gandhi says is true." 'Against war, one might say that it makes the victor stupid and the vanquished malicious." "However, for the sake of balance in this discussion, I offer in its favor that in producing these two effects it barbarizes, and so makes the combatants more natural. For culture, it is a sleep or a wintertime, and man emerges from it stronger for good and for evil.'"

"There you go, Fred, getting all esoteric on us again," interjected American historian Hermann Hagadorn, shaking his head. "I understand what Mr. Nietzsche is saying and agree with him to a point. A cultural sleep of reason can breed monsters. 'Consider that the bomb that fell on Hiroshima fell on America, too. It fell on no city, no munitions plants, no docks. It erased no church, vaporized no public buildings, reduced no man to his atomic elements. But it fell, it fell.'"

"I agree with Hermann," offered American anarchist/atheist Fred Woodworth, "and would like to offer another example. 'In an incredible perversion of justice, former soldiers who sprayed festeringly poisonous chemicals on Vietnam and now find today that they themselves have been damaged by them, appeal to the people for sympathy and charity. The effects of the defoliant Agent Orange are discussed at length, but not one single newspaper article or hearing that we are aware of has even mentioned the effects on the people who still live in those regions of Vietnam. It's as outlandish as if Nazis who gassed Jews now were to come forward and whine that the poisons that they utilized finally had made *them* sick. The staggering monstrousness goes unlaughed at and even unnoticed, as in a Kafka novel.'"

German Proverb: A Great War Leaves the Country with Three Armies -- an Army of Cripples, an Army of Mourners, and an Army of Thieves.

Buffing the stars on the epaulets of his jacket, General Dwight D. Eisenhower asserted, "I concur with Mr. Woodworth and the other Fred—Friedrich, that is. To tie this in with Ronald's original comment on cost, 'Every gun that is made, every warship launched, every rocket fired signifies, in the final sense, a theft from those who hunger and are not fed, those who are cold and are not clothed. This world in arms is not spending money alone. It is spending the sweat of its laborers, the genius of its scientists, the hopes of its children. This is not a way of life at all in any true sense. Under the clouds of war, it is humanity hanging on a cross of iron.'"

"Thank you, General Eisenhower," said American education reformer Abraham Flexner. "Through my work with the Carnegie and Rockefeller Foundations, I studied the finances of war in the early twentieth century. Now, as then, 'nations recently have been led to borrow billions for war; no nation has ever borrowed largely for education. Probably, no nation is rich enough to pay for both war and civilization. We must make our choice; we cannot have both.'"

Former Senator Charles Sumner of Massachusetts responded, "I agree with Abe. 'Give me the money that has been spent in war and I will clothe every man, woman, and child in an attire of which kings and queens will be proud. I will build a schoolhouse in every valley over the whole earth. I will crown every hillside with a place of worship consecrated to peace.'"

"I give my regards to Senator Sumner," said George Washington through his clattering wooden teeth. "He has underscored the point that the expense of war must produce some measurable benefit. Today, as in my own time, 'I do not mean to exclude altogether the idea of patriotism. I know it exists, and I know it has done much in the present contest. But I will venture to assert that a great and lasting war can never be supported on this principle alone. It must be aided by a prospect of interest, or some reward.'"

"In knowing and respecting George, my esteemed Whist partner," said English economist John Stuart Mill, "I hope that I understand him correctly in respect to a prospect of interest or some reward. I believe that 'war is an ugly thing, but not the ugliest of things. The decayed and degraded state of moral and patriotic feeling which thinks that nothing is worth war is much worse. The person who has nothing for which he is willing to fight, nothing which is more important than his own personal safety, is a miserable creature and has no chance of being free unless made and kept so by the exertions of better men than himself.'"

Pulling a lavender scarf from his coat sleeve and dobbing his nose gently, Oscar Wilde sniffed and said, "My fellow Britain, John Stuart Mill, has made a poignant case. However, the fundamental attraction to war remains perversely seated within the human psyche. 'As long as war is regarded as wicked, it will

97

always have its fascination. When it is looked upon as vulgar, it will cease to be popular.'"

"Mr. Mill and my drinking buddy Oscar Wilde have drawn well upon their education in the classics," said Sophocles, while tipping the laurel leaf on his head deferentially. "However, allow me to sum up these views in my own words. 'A mind at peace does not engender wars.'"

Recanted Jean-Paul Sartre, filled with ennui, "I have been sitting here listening to these elitist philosophical waxings of Messieurs Mill, Wilde, and Sophocles, However, the existential core of the matter is a much simpler matter of politics and class. 'When the rich wage war, it's the poor who die.'"

As the sunlight glinted on his Distinguished Flying Cross, George McGovern spoke up: "I concur with Monsieur Sartre. However, let me carry this concept one step further. The rich in power are old men while the poor at their mercy are young men. 'I'm fed up to the ears with old men dreaming up wars for young men to die in.'"

"Men, men, men, Mr. McGovern. It's always the same, George," shouted comedian Brett Butler, rolling her eyes. "'I would like it if men had to partake in the same hormonal cycles to which we're subjected monthly. Maybe that's why men declare war--because they have a need to bleed on a regular basis.'"

"Right on!" thundered Anglo-American novelist Lucy Ellmann. "I'm with sister Brett Butler. 'Men like war: they do not hold much sway over birth, so they make up for it with death. Unlike women, men menstruate by shedding other people's blood.'"

Returning from the buffet table, General Omar Bradley interjects, "Mr. McGovern, Ms. Butler, and Ms. Ellmann, this argument goes beyond class, age, and gender. It is a matter for all of humanity. 'The world has achieved brilliance without wisdom, power without conscience. Ours is a world of nuclear giants and ethical infants. We know more about war that we know about peace, more about killing that we know about living.'"

Musing over the promotional literature for Epcot's New World of Tomorrow given to him by his friend Walt Disney, H.G. Wells spoke from his smoking chair: "I must agree with General Bradley. 'If we don't end war, war will end us.'"

Fluffing his mop of hair, Albert Einstein smiled and said, "Good point, H.G." Einstein then turned to the assemblage and said, "I long have respected Mr. Wells's visions of our possible future. 'I do not know with what weapons World War III will be fought, but World War IV will be fought with sticks and stones.'"

While picking a piece of asparagus out of his teeth with a fishhook, Ernest Hemingway articulated, "Mr. Einstein. It seems that the human condition will never change. I would like to remind our group to 'never think that war, no matter how necessary, nor how justified, is not a crime.' By the way, Albert, is that a new suit?" Einstein, who still maintained a closet full of identical suits, shot Hemingway a deprecating look and said, "It's all relative."

Charon jumps in: "Gentlemen, gentlemen, let's preserve the niceties." Benjamin Disraeli broke in with, 'War is never a solution; it is an aggravation.'" "That's right," said Chairman Mao. "Spoken like a true politician. 'Politics is war without bloodshed while war is politics with bloodshed.'" Playing with his compass and set-square, Thomas Jefferson directed himself to the Chairman: "However, war powers inevitably rest with the politicians. 'The power of making war often prevents it.'"

"Most certainly, President Jefferson, nodded Vietnamese Zen Buddhist monk Thich Nhat Hanh. "Preventing war reflects wisdom. 'Preventing war is much better than protesting against the war. Protesting the war is too late.'"

"So," interjected French statesman Georges Clemenceau, "What we are hearing from Nhat Hanh and the others is that 'war is much too serious a matter to be entrusted to the military.'" Am I hearing correctly?

"I will concede your point, Monsieur Clemenceau," grunted Sir Winston Churchill while rolling around his cigar in his mouth. "However, as a politician, 'Never, never, never believe any war will be smooth and easy, or that anyone who embarks on the strange voyage can measure the tides and hurricanes he will encounter. The statesman who yields to war fever must realize that, once the signal is given, he is no longer the master of policy but the slave of unforeseeable and uncontrollable events.'"

A dapper John F. Kennedy chimed in: Ladies and gentlemen, for those in politics and those serving in the military, it seems that 'it is an unfortunate fact that we can secure peace only by preparing for war.'"

Jefferson takes the floor again: "That, Mr. Kennedy, is the responsibility that has come to rest with all branches of the government. 'The care of human life and happiness, and not their destruction, is the first and only object of good government.'"

Brushing the excess powder from his wig off of his shoulders, James Madison added, "Furthermore, my dear Mr. Jefferson, let us not forget exactly where that power of government rests. 'War ... should only be declared by the authority of the people, whose toils and treasures are to support its burdens, instead of the government, which is to reap its fruits.' Let me defer to my esteemed colleague Teddy Roosevelt, who is poking me in the side with his riding crop."

Adjusting his monocle and Rough Rider hat, Roosevelt swaggered to the center of the room and proclaimed loudly, "Thank you, Jim. Let me add a caveat to what Mr. Madison and Mr. Jefferson have just iterated, given the current state of political power in the United States. 'To announce that there must be no criticism of the president, or that we are to stand by the president, right or wrong, is not only unpatriotic and servile but is morally treasonable to the American public.' You have a comment, Bungalow Bill?"

Fuming, General William Westmoreland pointed his finger at Roosevelt and said bitingly, "What you just said is all well and good, Teddy. However, there must be controls. I remember that 'Vietnam was the first war ever fought without any censorship. Without censorship, things can get terribly confused in the public mind.' Why, during the recent Gulf War, a former colleague of mine at the Pentagon said, 'If we let people see that kind of thing, there would never again be any war.'"

Frowning at his fellow general, Omar Bradley replied sarcastically, "Thank you for your erudite comment, Bill. Of course, maybe that would not be a bad idea. After all, 'the way to win an atomic war is to make certain it never starts.' As I stated earlier this evening, 'We know more about killing than we know about living.' Let me add, 'We have grasped the mystery of the atom and rejected the Sermon on the Mount.'"

"Quite right, General Bradley," said Einstein. "'The release of atom power has changed everything except our way of thinking... [T]he solution to this problem lies in the heart of mankind. If only I had known, I should have become a watchmaker.'"

JFK responded, "The use of the atomic bomb was not your fault, Professor Einstein. As it was in the 1940s, the 1960s, and beyond, 'the basic problems facing the world today are not susceptible to a military solution.'"

"And this is especially true, President Kennedy, when speaking of such ideals as liberty and democracy," added Gandhi. "'Liberty and democracy become unholy when their hands are dyed red with innocent blood.'"

"Well put, Mr. Gandhi," smiled Kennedy approvingly. "However, let me continue to say this about that. 'The wave of the future is not the conquest of the world by a single dogmatic creed but the liberation of the diverse energies of free nations and free men.'"

Peace Is Not the Absence of War; It Is a Virtue, a State of Mind, a Disposition for Benevolence, Confidence, and Justice.

--Benedict (Baruch) De Spinoza

"I have become fed up with this serving of liberal tripe," bellowed a German-accented voice from the back. "'Naturally, the common people don't want war. That is understood. But, after all, it is the leaders of the country who determine policy, and it is always a simple matter to drag the people along, whether it is a democracy, or a fascist dictatorship, or a parliament, or a communist dictatorship. Voice or no voice, the people always can be brought to the bidding of the leaders. That is easy. All you have to do is to tell them they are being attacked, and denounce the pacifists for lack of patriotism and exposing the country to danger. It works the same in any country.'"

"Yes, Herr Goering," said Westmoreland. "However, Hermann, it seems that you have made my point. 'The military don't start wars. Politicians start wars.'"

Reentering the grand parlor from the "head," General Douglas MacArthur proclaimed, "I have returned. Yes, General Westmoreland; politicians such as these gentlemen declare war. However, it is we military creatures who must carry out the war. Personally, 'I know war as few other men now living know it, and nothing to me is more revolting. I long have advocated its complete abolition, as its very destructiveness on both friend and foe has rendered it useless as a method of settling international disputes.' Don't you agree, Otto?"

"Certainly I do, General MacArthur," replied Chancellor Von Bismark. "'Anyone who has ever looked into the glazed eyes of a soldier dying on the battlefield will think hard before starting a war.' Having been both sailor and politician, would not you agree, Lieutenant Kennedy?"

"Absolutely, Chancellor," said JFK. "'Mankind must put an end to war, or war will put an end to mankind.' To quote his Holiness, John Paul II, 'War should belong to the tragic past, to history: it should find no place on humanity's agenda for the future.'"

Benjamin Franklin, who had been making a tail for his latest kite by surreptitiously pulling bits of cloth off of Goering's frayed Nazi uniform, looked over his spectacles and said, "If I may interject, allow me to assert that 'all wars are follies, very expensive and very mischievous ones. In my opinion, there never was a good war or a bad peace. When will mankind be convinced and agree to settle their difficulties by arbitration?'"

French priest and writer Francois Fenelon added quietly, "'All wars are civil wars, because all men are brothers.'"

Pope John Paul II, who had been praying fervently for Goering and Sartre, addressed the group: "I thought I heard my name and words bandied about from across the room, Messrs. Kennedy, Franklin, and Fenelon. Allow me to sum up your insights. 'If you wish to be brothers, drop your weapons.'"

Charon returns to the podium: "'If you wish to be brothers, drop your weapons.' Thank you, your Holiness, for summing up our discussion so succinctly. I hope that our guests from the Land of the Living will carry these and all the other words back to their homes. To close our evening, I have asked Mr. Samuel Clemens, the great American writer and speaker, to recite a closing oration, his War Prayer. Let us all remember what we have discussed here on this houseboat on the River Styx. Mr. Clemens, if you would."

"Thank you, Charon. A few minutes ago, I was preparing myself while seated on the commode. While I was seated there, I read a piece of graffiti on the door of the stall. Apparently, it had been written sometime this evening by the German-born American physiologist Dr. Martin H. Fischer of our party. The verse read, 'The refuge of the morally, intellectually, artistically, and economically bankrupt is war.' That sentence moved me in more ways than one. So, in respect to Dr. Fischer and in all humbleness in the presence of this gathering of great minds, I dedicate my War Prayer, which, unfortunately, proves every bit as relevant today as when I myself lived:

"O Lord our God, help us tear their soldiers to bloody shreds with our shells; help us to cover their smiling fields with the pale forms of their patriot dead; help us to drown the thunder of the guns with the shrieks of their wounded, writhing in pain; help us to lay waste their humble homes with a hurricane of fire; help us to wring the hearts of their unoffending widows with unavailing grief; help us to turn them out roofless with their little children to wander unfriended the wastes of their desolated land in rags and hunger and thirst, sports of the sun flames of summer and the icy winds of winter, broken in spirit, worn with travail, imploring Thee for the refuge of the grave and denied it."

An Afterglow for Economists

The Dismal Science?

In this book, we have applied economics--what English historian and essayist Thomas Carlyle described as "the dismal science".

"Not a 'gay science,' I should say, like some we have heard of; no, a dreary, desolate, and, indeed, quite abject and distressing one; what we might call, by way of eminence, the dismal science."

--Thomas Carlyle, "Occasional Discourse on the Negro Question," (*Fraser's Magazine for Town and Country*, London, 1849)

In a derogatory and perhaps retaliatory manner, Carlyle labeled economics as the "dismal science" as he promoted the reintroduction of the British slave trade. Carlyle argued that slavery actually was morally superior to the market forces of supply and demand promoted by economists. In his responsive essay "The Negro Question," English economist John Stuart Mill subsequently attacked Carlyle's infamous view (*Fraser's Magazine for Town and Country*, 1850).

The Economist as Zoloft Poster Child?

Non-economist friends assert that economists are a gloomy lot. Other less kind critics view our field as one that attracts the chronically depressed. Granted, we sometimes may party like it's 1984. However, bereft of colorful characters we do not remain. To illustrate, the nineteenth-century English economist Jeremy Bentham could not have gone to his reward without some sense of humor. Leaving a large endowment to University College London (UCL), Bentham set forth in his will that his remains be wheeled solemnly into the Council Room at the school so that he may take his place at regular meetings of the College

Council. Since his demise, the minutes of the meetings always have recorded him as "present but not voting."

According to UCL, "Bentham had originally intended that his head should be part of the Auto-Icon [the display of his remains housed in a wooden cabinet], and for ten years before his death carried around in his pocket the glass eyes which were to adorn it." The time came to preserve Bentham's head for posterity (through a process of desiccation practiced by the New Zealand Maoris). However, the process, as the UCL notes, "went disastrously wrong, robbing the head of most of its facial expression, and leaving it decidedly unattractive." Thereafter, the college substituted a wax head. For some years, the real head, with its glass eyes, reposed on the floor between Bentham's legs in the Auto-Icon, which is located at the end of the South Cloisters of the main building of UCL. Unfortunately, Bentham's head became the target of a roving gang of economics students from King's College London who stole it and held it for ransom. Apparently, according to the UCL, the last straw came "when the head was discovered in the front quadrangle being used for soccer practice." Henceforth, Bentham's noggin was removed to more secure storage: a vault in the Archeology Department. Today, Jeremy Bentham's fully attired skeleton, surmounted with the wax head, can be seen as he sits in the lobby case.[84] Tea time is over. Back on your heads!

Notes:

1 State Motto of Michigan, adopted 1835.

2 Universal Pictures, 1985.

3 Henriette Mertz, The Mystic Symbol: Mark of the Michigan Mound Builders, Global, 1986; revised edition, Hayriver Press, 2004.

4 W. B. Hinsdale, Primitive Man in Michigan and Archaeological Atlas of Michigan, University of Michigan Press, 1925 and 1931, respectively)

5 Eleusis Alesia, private printing, 1936, op. cit.; Francis Hitching, The Mysterious World: An Atlas of the Unexplained, Holt, Rinehart, and Winston, 1978.

6 Henry Lincoln, The Holy Place: Sauniere and the Decoding of the Mystery of Rennes-le-Chateau, Arcade, 1991.

7 Vivian M. Baulch, Detroit News, 6 June 1997.

8 quote from the song "Silver Winter's Morn" from Aessence by John Sase, Freezer Theatre Records, 1985.

9 World Futures, Vol. 37, 1993.

10 Brookings Institution Press, 1997.

11 Woodrow Wilson Center press, 1993.

12 Island Press, 1995.

13 Detroit Journal of Economics & Law, Vol. 2, No.1, 1999.

14 "Amid Slump, Real-Estate Agents Hang up Their Blazers," WSJ, 7 February 2007.

15 "In Home-Lending Push, Banks Misjudged Risk," WSJ, 8 February 2007.

16 Lombard Street: A Description of the Money Market (Scribner, Armstrong, 1874).

17 Wall Street Journal, 14 March 2007.

18 "Subprime Fears Spread, Sending Dow Down 1.97%," 14 March 2007.

19 "Orlando Condo Converter Will Face Federal Fraud Charge," 18 October 2006.

20 20th Century Fox, 1998.

21 "For One Condo Developer, Boom Ends with Arrest," 15 March 2007.

22 "Mortgage Shakeout May Roil CDO Market, 12 March 2007.

23 quoted in the Robert Greenwald film Wal-Mart: The High Cost of Low Price (The Disinformation Company Ltd., 2005)

24 Good Jobs First, www.goodjobsfirst.org.

25 "What Business Should Expect in Next Congress," 9 November 2006.

26 "Oak Park Wants to Recoup Tax Break," 7 December 2006.

27 "A New Way to Sue," 13 October 2006.

28 Brave New Films, 2005.

29 Berrett-Koehler Publishers, 2006.

30 "Plan to Build in Northville Gains," 7 October 2006.

31 www.fra.org.

32 Belknap, 2007.

33 5 April 2007.

34 Detroit News, 16 January 2007.

35 "Mortgage Meltdown," Wall Street Journal, 21 March 2007.

36 www.mbaa.org, 11 April 2007.

37 www.askmerrill.ml.com.

38 www.aei.org.

39 AEI Press, 2006.

40 W.W. Norton; 2007.

41 We refer the reader to Bethany McLean and Peter Elkind's book Enron: The Smartest Guys in the Room, Portfolio Hardcover, 2003.

42 www.hispanicbusiness.com.

43 www.nahrep.org.

44 Paramount Pictures, 1974.

45 Cartier Productions, 1971.

46 www.mcso.org.

47 "Bond Investors' Lament," 3 April 2007.

48 City Light Books, 1977.

49 PBS, 2008.

50 Universal Pictures, 1954.

51 Dialog Press, 2008.

52 Public Affairs, 2008.

53 see Michael Douglas in Oliver Stone's film Wall Street, 1987.

54 to quote Blanche DuBois in Tennessee Williams' play A Streetcar Named Desire, 1947.

55 How to Call Michael Keaton's Character in the Film Beetlejuice, Warner Bros, 1988.

56 Jeff Goldblum to Will Smith in Independence Day, 20th Century Fox, 1996.

57 Paramount, 1994.

58 1975, Freezer Theatre Records, 1985.

59 Columbia Records, 1968

60 "General Motors's Massive Negative Equity," http://stefanmikarlsson.blogspot.com.

61 Copyright 1975, recorded, Freezer Theatre Records, 1985. Dr. Sase's original recordings of "Winter Song" and "Industrial Age" can be heard in full at www.plumstreetmusic.com.

62 GM Media Web site, http://media.gm.com/division/gmac/.

63 GM Inside News, www.gminsidenews.com.

64 Editions du Seuil, 1955.

65 "GM Taps Pension for Billions: Questions Arise from Use of Money for Buyouts, VEBA Trust," 1 March 2009.

66 United States v. E.I. du Pont de Nemours & Co., 366 U.S. 316 [1961].

67 MCA Records, 1998.

68 "'Surgical' Bankruptcy Possible for G.M.," NYT, 12 April 2009.

69 autonews.com.

70 npr.org.

71 Amphenol Corp. v. Shandler (In re Insilco Technologies, Inc.), Adv. Proc. No. 05-52403 (Bankr. D. Del. Sept. 18, 2006).

72 Bankruptcy Section 363 Sales: Buyers Beware of "Free and Clear" Sales of Non-debtor Subsidiaries, 24 October 2006, wilmerhale.com.

73 Restated Certificate of Incorporation, 1 March 2004, Division I: Common stock, [c] Liquidation Rights.

74 New York Times, 2 March 1993, "Company News; General Motors Stock Redemption to Cost $265 Million."

75 cnbc.com.

76 NBC Television, 2009.

77 MSNBC.com, 1 June 2009.

78 20th Century Fox, 1987.

79 "Who's Sticking up for GM: Ralph Nader."

80 e.g. Dark Secrets: Inside the Bohemian Grove, 2000.

81 see Hugh Jackman in the Stephen Sommers' film of the same name, 2004.

82 Sun Mt. Chronicles, 8 December 2001.

83 Harper & Brothers, 1895.

84 www.ucl.ac.uk/Bentham-Project/site_images/auto_il.gif

www.ingramcontent.com/pod-product-compliance
Lightning Source LLC
Chambersburg PA
CBHW071227170526
45165CB00003B/1022